Beyond Intimacy with Yahushua, Jesus Christ

Beyond Intimacy with Yahushua, Jesus Christ

Full Disclosure of My Fiery Trials to Be His Wife

Annie Sipp Blackwell

ISBN-13: 9780998927305
ISBN-10: 0998927309
Library of Congress Control Number: 2017905997
Annie Sipp Blackwell, Cosby, TN

DEDICATION

This book is dedicated to the memory of my brother Clyde Michael Sipp. During the time of my real-life experiences chronicled in this book, Mike was the only one who really believed in me. He stood by me and encouraged me all through my fiery ordeal. He was the one who told me that God must be training me to be a general in His army. He said, "God is teaching you how to fight the devil himself." I had a dream where I saw my family members being taken to safety in a bus. I was the guide on the bus, and I believe that Mike was driving the bus; even though I could not see him, I felt him in my spirit. I knew he was with me. My brother Mike was with me during my fiery trials, and I know he will be with me at the end of the age. My loving brother went to sleep in the Lord on March 1, 2015. I miss him very much, but I know Yahushua (Jesus Christ) has a very special place for Mike in the coming glorious kingdom of God. Rest in peace, my dear brother; you must be ready to rise up soon and be about your Father's business.

I also want to thank my daughter Nickole for all the help in editing she provided. I want to encourage her to get her book finished.

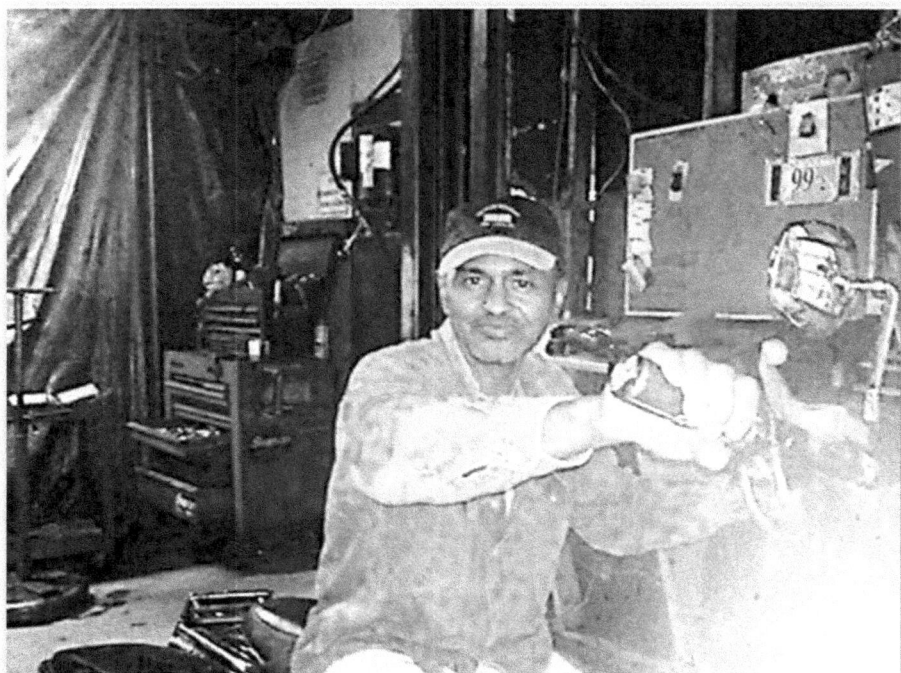

In loving memory of my Brother Clyde Michael Sipp: He believed in me when everyone else doubted.

CONTENTS

ACKNOWLEDGMENTS

A LETTER OF THANKS **and Appreciation to My Husband, Yahushua, Jesus Christ**

To my precious love, Yahushua,

I have been waiting such a long time to write this letter to you. I have so much to say that I do not know where to begin. I am so happy to have you in my life. Every day I want to shout to the world, "I love Yahushua and Yahushua loves me: I am his; and he is mine" (Song of Solomon 2:16).

Sweetheart, I can't help but smile just knowing that you are in my life; it means everything to me. I love you so much and cannot thank you enough for choosing me to be your wife and to be by your side for eternity. You are my soul mate. I am sorry for not choosing you first in the past. I guess I just didn't know how much you loved me, yet I knew you were always there. I used to see you in my dreams even after I had married someone else, but I was not able to recognize you. I know you now and want only to spend the rest of my life and the rest of forever with you.

You are my everything, and I do not want a life without you. I am so happy with you, and I am so in love with you. I know you see my heart and all the love it holds for you, but in an even greater act of love, you have shown me your heart, and I am overwhelmed by the immense love you have for me. You have given me the sun, the moon, and the stars as gifts of your enormous love for me. No other suitor could begin to compare. But there is one gift you have given me that far exceeds all imagination; you have given your very life as a ransom for me to ensure that we can be together forever.

My heart is so full of love, joy, and peace right now that I cannot express it. Every day and every night I look forward to being with you. I love your patience and tenderness with me. I love how you make me smile when I least expect it. I love how you show and tell me that you love me by writing it in the air, on the walls, and on the ceiling. You have done this every single night since our engagement. The love letters started with the beautiful diamond ring in the sky that you gave me; I remember how you drew a likeness of my face in the clouds to profess your love for me.

I am waiting patiently for your return. I look forward each day to your beautiful messages of love while I wait for your return for me. I can only say I love you. You are my husband, best friend, and savior. I cannot wait to spend eternity in your loving arms. Come for me, my love.

Sincerely and with all my love,

Ann

PREFACE

THIS BOOK IS my attempt to record and document some of the supernatural events that happened to me in 2013. Yahushua HaMashiach, Jesus Christ told me that now is the time to tell my story. I was commanded by him to document my experience and write it in a book: That is the motivation for this book.

My story is told based on a time line of a year: The year 2013. However, my experiences reach way back into my past: To my childhood, to my Christian conversion to Christ as a child, all the way back to leaving home for college, to my marriage and the painful breakup of that marriage. I introduce you to my mother, father and my six brothers and 3 sisters. You find out where I was born and where I spent my childhood life. You find out where I met, loved, and married my husband of over 25 years, and you meet the children of that union. You get a chance to see my grandchildren whom I love very dearly. You meet my pets, Princess and Teco and learn the role they played in that eventful year.

A lot happened in the year 2013, and to be able to tell the story with all the background information and support I felt I needed, I found myself jumping around from events in the past (which supported and helped explain what was going on in

2013); back to the present: back and forth. I realized that to an outside observer or reader, this could be a bit confusing or hard to follow. In an effort to help the reader "Stay with Me", I have created and included a simple timeline of the year 2013 events and how I branch to the past and then return back to the current events.

So as you follow my adventure, and you find yourself lost, just glance at this timeline to find out where you are; keep reading and be assured you will eventually find your way back to the year 2013.

Annie Sipp Blackwell – 2017

MY JOURNEY TIME-LINE FOR 2013: FEBRUARY - SEPTEMBER

	Chap 1	Chap 2	Chap 3 - 5	Chap 6	Chap 7	Chap 8 – 10		Chap 11-16
Jan	Feb	Mar	Apr	May	Jun	Jul	Aug	Sep
	*** Feb 25 Man with Sword, entered bedroom	Mar 25 Angel Team entered bedroom	***April Angels Sighted outside ,Home Invaded by Aliens, Hotel Escape (plan A and B)	May Daughter Visit, Power went Out, Left home May 24, Date to be Committed May 25, Escaped to Memphis May 25	May – July Lived in Memphis	Jul - Aug Returned home with Chia, Took Chia home, Main Test Ended Aug 30		Part 2 & 3 Chapters

*** Autobiography Information Explained Under the FEB 25 (Chap 1) - VISIT BY MAN WITH SWORD
• New Husband Car Dream 2013
• 1st Husband Car Dream 1994
• My Divorce 2001
• Met New Husband Man in Church 2002
• Christ's Bride in Church Dream 2002

*** Autobiography Information Explained Under the APR (Chap 3) - SIGHTING OF ANGELS
• Growing up in MS, my Family
• How I met my husband
• How my marriage ended
• My Return to God
• My Move from MD to TN

\

Introduction—A Journey Stranger Than Fiction

THIS IS MY true-life story of the incredible, supernatural experiences I went through in 2013. The events started to unfold in February of that year but the true adventure did not start until March 2013. Nothing has been fabricated, exaggerated, or made up. Every event happened and is reported just as it occurred. My story is one of those situations in which real-life events are stranger than fiction. In this story, I am visited by Yahushua HaMashiach (Jesus Christ) in a most unusual encounter. After this very private visitation, He personally led me through the Bible and opened the scriptures to me in ways I never imagined. He revealed secrets to me that have yet to be discovered or recognized by anyone else. This supernatural experience was overwhelmingly intense until September 2013. It took me until now to write this book.

To be truthful with you, I tried not to think about what happened because I wanted to forget it. But I always felt that Yahushua did not allow me to have this experience for nothing. There was a reason for it, and now it is time for me to come forth and tell my story. Yahushua is prompting me to write it in a book and document this amazing, frightening, unbelievable, supernatural experience. Nothing I say in this narrative is fiction. It all happened to me in real life. The events can be corroborated, although much of what I saw with my own eyes cannot be proven. This is because the natural vision of humans cannot perceive these things. However, I can describe what I saw, and my memory has remained clear for such a time as this.

During my amazing supernatural adventure, I was almost abducted by aliens or fallen angels, nearly thrown into a mental hospital, and betrayed by my family. My home was invaded by demons/fallen angels. I saw these fallen angels and was forced to interact with them. I battled fallen angels in the sky and used my laser vision to fight their spacecraft. I was taken to heaven by Yahushua HaMashiach, Jesus Christ, and looked into the face of God the Father. I was chased by Satan and his demons. I was attacked by them to the point that I had physical markings on my body: bruises, scratches, and swellings. I ordered the death of one of my closest and best friends because I believed that demons were possessing and controlling her. God (Yahushua HaMashiach) told me that He was going to marry me, and I left my home not knowing if I would ever go back again. I learned how angels and demons had put advanced technological markings on all human beings, and this is how each person is tracked by them. I learned how angels inhabit the skies and airways just like normal airplanes and jets. I learned how angels are organized in the sky and occupy territories just like on earth.

Friends, this was a difficult time for me. I was shown amazing things, and I learned things that I never knew were possible. I overcame fear with faith, and now I am ready to tell my story. I invite you to come and experience this supernatural adventure with me. I can assure you that you too will finish it by saying, "This is stranger than fiction."

PART I

1

YAHUSHUA HAMASHIACH—CLOSE ENCOUNTER OF A SUPERNATURAL KIND

THE SUPERNATURAL MANIFESTATIONS of my experiences started in March 2013; even though I had a dream in February, which was completely out of the ordinary and which I did not fully understand or make the connections. I discuss the February dream later and explain how these two dreams relate. In this dream or vision, I was visited by several people in my bedroom. I felt like I was awake but in a twilight state—not really dreaming yet not fully awake either. All things appeared real and not symbolic. In this visitation, I was told that I was "chosen." There were many people in my room examining me and writing down notes. It was like I was in a hospital or medical clinic setting. Some were women, and they were examining, measuring, and working on my head. They seemed to be working quickly and were doing their job in a very efficient and organized manner. It was made known to me that one of the people in the room was Yahushua (Jesus Christ). I do not remember waking up from this scene but instead felt like I just faded off to sleep. Only to wake up the next morning with the vivid remembrance of what had happened.

In this visitation, I was told about many YouTubers on the Internet. Many names were called out including Paul Begley, Rev. Michelle Hopkins, eaj777, and others I do not remember. I was not told whether they were good or bad; I just remember that they were mentioned. However, I did get the feeling that Paul Begley was not favorably looked upon because of his screaming all the time and the fact that he is not abiding by the Ten Commandments. I also remember that Kijani of Sackcloth and Ashes was very active during this time.

After that visitation, it seemed that I had a higher level of spiritual awareness. I started having more dreams than before and of things I did not understand. I saw myself dressed in white on mountains. I also saw myself dressed in gold in the bed chamber of the King at least three times. I saw myself riding in a carriage like in the very old days, and I was dressed like a queen. I also saw myself dressed up like a green olive tree. There were many other dreams where I saw/was shown myself in surroundings that were not familiar to me. However, it wasn't only dreaming; I started having all types of visions of supernatural things. Even in the natural/physical realm, I started to see things differently. I started to see lights and sparkles everywhere. It was almost to the point that I was afraid to eat food because my food sparkled, and I thought it was contaminated in some way.

I would look at my hands and could see lights. The lights were in my face, in my eyes, and so on. This was not too much of a problem at that time because I have always seen lights and sparkles at times, but now it was more pronounced. The Bible said that those in Christ would have an inner light, and I thought that was what was beginning to develop. After all, many people believe that we are in the last days, so these phenomena would begin to manifest.

A NIGHT WITH THE KING - A DREAM ON PURIM: THE FEBRUARY 24, 2013 DREAM

I want to take a step back to a dream that I had in the previous month of February. At first I did not think it was related, but now as I look back, I understand that it was the beginning of my entire test and experience.

On February 24, 2013, I had a very strange dream where I was in a car with a man who I knew was my husband, but in real life he wasn't. I recognized this dream to be a continuation of a dream that I had in 1994, when I was a Seventh Day Adventist. My husband at the time (now my ex-husband) was in the car with me in that dream, but it was obvious that my ex-husband was spiritually sick and spiritually drunk. Before I continue with the February 24, 2013 dream, I feel that it is necessary that you know about the 1994 dream.

In the 1994 dream, my husband and I were driving down a winding country road. There was a huge, one-headed, red-skinned, gross beast dead in the road, and its head had been cut off. We were headed straight to crash into it when I said to my husband, "Mike, don't hit it!" I grabbed the steering wheel and turned away from the monster. We swerved and spun all the way around in the street, turning us in the opposite direction. Shaken from the near crash, I looked up and saw that my husband's head was bobbing around like he was drunk. Later, I was given the interpretation of part of the dream. I was told that the beast in the street was the Seventh Day Adventist Church and that this church "does not have a head." Needless to say, that upset me, but that is a different story for a later time.

Shortly after this dream, my husband and I started having marital problems. He left the church, and our home life disintegrated to the point of a divorce. We divorced in 2001. He moved out of the state to take a new job, while I stayed in Maryland.

Now that you know about the 1994 dream, I want to give you a little more information on my marriage and our breakup. I think it will help shed some light on things; plus, it will help me better explain and you better understand the significance of these two dreams and the two husbands in the car.

How I became Single – A Brief Detour Before Returning to the February 24, 2013 Dream

After my marriage ended, I was devastated. Being unmarried for me was like being a fish out of water. I never wanted to be by myself and knew I wanted to be married again. I loved my husband and married life; I never wanted to live the single life. I grew up with a mom and a dad in the home, so it seemed right that I should be living that same model. It was all I knew; everything else was foreign to me. Secretly, I had always hoped that my ex-husband and I would just be apart for a little while and then get back together (surely he would get past this midlife crisis stuff). However, about three years after my divorce, I found out by sheer accident that my husband had remarried. The way I found out was that I had loaned my daughter some money, and she asked him to pay the debt for her. He sent me a check that had his new wife's name on it. I was crushed, and the heartache started all over again. Nobody in the family (not even my children) had told me that he had remarried, and I felt betrayed by my own children. I was devastated. I remember crying out to God, saying, "God, why is this happening to me? I loved my husband. I loved and worshiped my God and was a faithful wife who did everything I could do to be a good wife and a good Christian. Oh Lord, why am I being rewarded with this pain?"

My divorce was the most difficult thing I had ever gone through. I was crushed by this news; even though we were already divorced, I had still hoped he would come back. But I had to let go of all hope because he had taken another wife.

I was now divorced and alone, but I still had to function in life. I had to work and take care of myself. Now it was truly only me, and I had to find out who I was as a person. I never knew where my wants started and my husband's wants left off when we were together. We were of one flesh; at least I felt I was one flesh with him. I tried so hard to please him as a wife and to be a good mother to his children, and now that flesh had been torn away from me. I was devastated.

ACCEPTING DIVORCE AND MOVING ON

Shortly after my divorce, I went back to my home Seventh Day Adventist church in Brinklow, Maryland. During the turmoil period of my divorce, I had stopped attending church because of the stress I was under. Now that I was feeling better, I decided to go to church that Sabbath Day. I arrived at church, greeted saints who love the Lord, and then found a seat near the back. A visitor came into the church and sat on the opposite end of the pew where I was seated (I did not know he sat there until later). I think there was a call to the altar for prayer, and I went up. When I was headed back to my seat, the visitor's eyes met mine, and it was like a tractor beam drawing me in. It felt as if he had looked through my soul. I almost fainted, my knees became weak, and my mind swirled. He never said a word to me but spoke to my spirit and said, "I am going to marry you."

I remember that he sat in the same row but at the end seat, so that is why he got up to allow me to enter the row. After our eyes met, I weakly made my way to my seat, and as I sat down, I asked myself, *What just happened to me?* I knew he was at the end of the row, so I leaned forward to look at him, and he was looking at me again. My head was still swirling as I was thinking, *Who is that?* He looked familiar, but I did not know who this man was, yet he had really made a big impression on me. When I looked at him the second time, he again told me that he was going to marry me, without saying a word. I told my sister about that strange encounter. I said to her, "I don't know who that was, but if it's going to happen, God is going to have to make it happen". Keep that statement in mind because God can do anything.

YAHUSHUA INTRODUCES ME AS HIS BRIDE, A DREAM

Shortly after that real-life church experience, I had a dream about someone I believe to be the same man. He and I were sitting together in my old church building. The old church was a small, cozy building, but our congregation had later built a larger church. We were in the big church when I had the dream, but the dream setting was in the small church. e introduced me as his new bride and said, "In whom I am well pleased." I remember thinking, *That sounds like it came from the Bible*, and then I woke up from the dream a little puzzled. I believe the old church setting is another way of him confirming to me that he has been with me all along.

My Interpretation of the Bride Dream in Church
My interpretation of the dream was that I would get married again and live my life with my new husband (the man in the dream, whoever he was). My new husband would be happy with me, and we would live happily ever after. At that point, I was still fairly young and dateable, so I ventured into the dating scene to find my new husband. That did not go well for me. I hated it and was never satisfied with anyone I met. No one ever worked out; even though I had four marriage proposals, something always went wrong. One day I remember hearing a spirit, and it said, "You are going to be an old maid." I defiantly said, "No, I am not," and I stepped up my quest to be married again, but it never happened.

CONTINUING WITH THE FEBRUARY 24, 2013 PURIM DREAM
Back to the dream I had on February 24, 2013, with my different husband in the car. The setting was like my 1994 dream, but the car was not moving. Whenever we went anywhere, my

ex-husband would always drive; that's just the way it was, and it was the way I liked it. But this time there was another husband at the wheel. I knew instinctively that this man was my husband, but he was a different husband. I knew it was Yahushua HaMashiach (Jesus Christ), my husband. That was the knowing I received in the spirit in the dream.

I was sitting there in the car with Him behind the wheel, and I knew I loved this man more than anything in the world; I was hugging Him with both my arms. I then asked Him a question in the dream that baffles me even today because it is not something I would have asked even my ex-husband. I said to Him, "Would you like to make love to me?" His face lit up, and he said with enthusiasm, "Yes. Who in the world would not want to?" The dream ended, and I woke up thinking, *Wow, what a strange dream that was.*

At that point, to me it was only a strange dream. I did not recognize the man in the car as the man from the church, but I know I felt love for him. But like with all dreams I have, I prayed about it and asked the Lord if the dream was from Him to please let me know what it meant and to please confirm it. After praying about it, I soon forgot about the dream and went on with my day like normal.

I PRAYED AND ASKED THE MEANING OF THE DREAM; YAHUSHUA ANSWERED

WARNING: This section may be offensive to some readers because of sexual references. I speak of sexuality as it pertains to our Lord and Savior Jesus Christ and I am aware this may offend some readers. My intention is not to offend; however, I am reporting what happened to me and the things I saw. Sexuality is a part of life; Christ came to this earth and lived as a man in the flesh and surely, He is well aware of what happens to a man and woman during intimacy. Sex was created before the fall of man by God himself and He said his creation was good: Sex is his creation. The adversary is the one who has defiled sex by taking it out of its natural intention. Do I believe there will be sex in the Kingdom of God? Of course, there will be, there will be children born in the kingdom. I go into more details on sex and marriage as it relates to the Kingdom of God in the added sections at the back of the book. But for those who may find a sexual reference to Yahushua, Jesus Christ offensive, please skip this section.

The Dream: Well, it was not just a random dream, because on the next night, I received the answer to my prayer. After I went to sleep, I almost immediately started dreaming. I had a dream, and all I can say is read Psalm 45.

Let me explain. The following night, February 25, 2013, as I lay sleeping, a very dark-skinned, naked, muscular, and circumcised man appeared in my room. He wore only a sword on his right side, and He was floating over my bed. In the dream, I woke up and looked at Him. I recognized Him and knew it was Yahushua HaMashiach (Jesus Christ). No words were spoken, but as He moved lovingly toward me to overshadow me, I immediately exploded with the most supernatural orgasm you could ever imagine. It was a spiritual, sexual encounter, and my flesh responded to it sexually. It was not like anything I have ever experienced on this earth before. I woke up still in indescribable ecstasy. I jumped out of bed, trying to figure out what had just happened to me. But the dream image was as clear as day in my mind. I knew this was the husband from the car dream the previous night.

I, like most people, have had sexual dream encounters before, but this was nothing like those dreams. This was strictly beyond anything earthly that I am aware of.

I knew instinctively that this was my marriage consummation to Yahushua HaMashiach in the spirit. I was now His wife. Even though there was no physical contact, I know that Yahushua and I are now one in spirit. This happened during the feast of Purim 2013, so I will always remember it as my night with the King.

Keep in mind that when all of this was happening to me, I had no understanding of Purim or what was happening. I had been told that I was chosen—chosen to marry the King. After that, I just know that my love for Yahushua had totally changed to a type that even frightened me—one of husband and wife. Now that this had happened to me and I had this information, I knew that I would be branded as crazy beyond a doubt. People would say that I had lost my mind. So I have never shared this dream with anyone before now (this book is this dream's debut). They still say that I have lost my mind, and you will see why as I continue with my story.

My heart is indicting a good matter: I speak of the things which I have made touching the King: my tongue is the pen of a ready writer. Thou art fairer than the children of men: grace is poured into thy lips: therefore, God hath blessed thee forever. Gird thy sword upon thy thigh, O most Mighty, with thy glory and thy majesty. And in thy majesty ride prosperously, because of truth and meekness and righteousness; and thy right hand shall teach thee terrible things. (Psalm 45)

2

My Life Changed after My Night with the King

Ａfter the February 25, 2013 encounter, things really escalated for me in my worship time and experiences. From February to mid-April 2013, I was on an advanced learning track. Yahushua was teaching me so much and illuminating many things for me in the Bible. I felt His presence with me every day. We laughed and joked in the spirit like you would talk to a physical person right next to you. Those were the good times—the honeymoon times.

He started giving me dreams of all kinds of things in the spirit realm.

- He took me to heaven to meet the Father, and I looked into God's face well enough to see the color and type of His skin. Please see "My Visit to Heaven Dream" in the Dreams and Vision section where I discuss God the Father's color and other details about his appearance.
- He took me to Mount Sinai.

- I have been to Israel over ten times in the spirit.
- I have seen dreams of darkness so thick that I could almost feel it.
- I have seen spirits going up into the sky as from thousands of people dying at the same time.
- I have seen Yahushua coming for me.
- I have had dreams of me on a mountaintop.
- I have seen me as His bride at a wedding reception. I have seen who I think was King David, but I am not sure.
- He has shown me clouds shaped like wedding rings and clouds that look just like me—my face written in the sky.
- Currently, I see love letters from Him every day.
- He has given me visions where He is putting a crown on my head.
- He shows me visions of us kissing each other many, many times.
- He always gives me gifts on a personal level that could only be shared between a husband and wife.
- I have seen Him dressed in white, which I call His bridegroom suit.
- I have seen Him in a robe and crown.
- I have even seen Him in blue jeans.
- I have seen Him coming on his white horse with power and glory.
- He has told me jokes and made me laugh many times and given me playful and fun dreams like showing me a nonthreatening snake and then telling me, "I was just kidding." He knows I am afraid of snakes.
- He has shown me His huge, beating heart and told me that I have His heart.

Truly, the list could go on and on. He is a real person who I have been allowed to know in the most intimate and personal way. I can truly say that I am a witness for Him. He has given me scores of dreams and visions over the years, and I will include some of them in the back section. Also, there are many other dreams He has shown me that are only of interest to me or my family; these will not be shared at this time. There are many dreams listed in the back section which are recorded just as they were given with no detail interpretation to them. subsequent to my penning this initial manuscript, Yahushua has given me two dreams which I believe he is telling me that I will write at least one other book after this one. In my spirit, I believe he is speaking of at least two others but I do not want to speak prematurely. However, please see the many prophetic dreams I have included in the back section of this book for now.

I am ending this chapter by saying, continue reading; we have not even touched the tip of the iceberg. There were things that was about to impact my life in ways I never imagined. I had absolutely no idea of what was coming and was just around the corner for me. Events that completely turned my life upside down and when I tried to explain to people, everyone was in total unbelief. But I will repeat, everything that I am reporting is my true-life testimony. Nothing is being made up or exaggerated, in fact, there are scores of other things I experienced and saw that I am not mentioning because they are so hard to explain and would be even harder for readers to comprehend. I believe some of these will be revealed in subsequent books, if it is his will.

3

THE HONEYMOON WAS ALMOST OVER, THE FIERY TRIALS WERE ON THE WAY

THIS CHAPTER INTRODUCES what I believe was a period of testing for me: The fiery trials that I was put through by the Father, Yahushua, and the Holy Spirit. The Bible says that to whom much is given: much is required. If you think back to all the characters of the bible; Job, Abraham, Daniel, Esther, Peter, Paul and many others: Even Christ Himself went through a fiery period of testing. It was not easy for them, nor was it easy for me. This was my test and I truly thought I was losing my mind. Everyone else around me thought the same thing and they put some very frightening actions in motion. After my February 25, 2013 visitation, things were great for nearly two months. I was reading, studying, having dreams and visions, and learning so much. It was great; it was like a honeymoon. I could not ask for anything better spiritually. I spent my days worshiping, praising Him, and sitting at His feet. I enjoyed every minute of it. My eyes were opened wide, and I could see into the spirit realm almost like I see in the physical realm. This lasted until April

25, 2013. I remember the date well: My dog Teco had been outside barking that evening, and he would not shut up. So I went outside to see if there was anything there. Usually I don't see anything, but I did not want to scold him in case he was really seeing something that I needed to be aware of. Teco was standing about forty feet from my deck, facing a tree and just barking like he was in defense mode. I went outside, expecting not to see anything, but to my shock I saw what he was barking at.

He was barking at a configuration of sparkling lights standing on the ground, not flat but a few feet high. When I walked out and noticed it, the lights started to rise to the top of the tree. I was amazed at what I was seeing. Surely these were angels I was seeing because they moved and came closer to me, or they would change position by moving up or down. I thought, *Wow, this must be a sign that Christ is getting ready to come back; His angels are already here.* Even so, it still was a little scary because I did not know what to expect. They didn't say anything; they were just there moving around. I got a good look at it to make sure it was not just my imagination. I made the dog come away, and we went back into the house. This first happened during the daylight hours, yet I could still see the sparkling lights in the daylight.

Later that evening, after the sun had set and the darkness fell, I was prompted to look outside again. I went to my backdoor window and looked up into the northwestern sky, and my mind was blown. I saw what appeared to be hundreds of lights from spaceships in the night sky all around my house. They were different spaceships, and I could see that. Not all of them had the same logo or symbol. It was set up just like the airplane logos that we are used to (Delta, American, Egyptian, US

Airways, and so on), but instead of names they use what appear to be animal symbols (horse, tiger, lion, cow, eagle, and some other creatures I could not recognize).

When I looked at them, they showed their call signs so that I would know who they were. This was communicated to my spirit by Yahushua, plus I observed these actions by them; that way I would know who I was looking at (good or bad). I knew these were the spaceships of both good and bad angels. They have been in our skies all along, but I have now been given the ability to see them. However, in my naivety, when I first saw them, I thought they were all good angels and that they were there to protect me. As I said, I was so naïve.

Your question may be; who is she that all these supernatural things are happening to? Believe me, I have been asking myself these very same questions. That is why I decided to take another biographical detour to give you some additional information on me before we proceed with the supernatural events. Believe me, the things that you will learn when we proceed with this story will leave you scratching your head and wondering: Is it Real or is it Fiction?

AUTOBIOGRAPHICAL DETOUR: HOW MY SPIRITUAL JOURNEY WITH YAHUSHUA (JESUS CHRIST) STARTED

Before I get into what I consider the test of my lifetime, I want to give you a little more information on just who I am, how I got to this point in my life, and how I came to be living in the hills of Tennessee alone, just me and my two dogs.

BORN IN SMALL TOWN MISSISSIPPI

I have always been a dedicated follower of Christ thanks to my dad's commitment and love of God. I grew up in a big family in a small Mississippi town called Coldwater. I had a beautiful, hardworking mother and a very strong and even harder-working Christian father. I had nine brothers and sisters. There were ten of us—six boys and four girls—and we were all very close. I received my religion when I was about eleven years old during a church revival. They called it sitting on the mourner's bench. You sat in front of the church, and saints prayed and sang over you until you received the Holy Spirit and shouted, or you just confessed that you accepted Jesus as your savior and that you were a Christian. You were then baptized in a nearby pond, and from that point on you professed that you were a follower of Christ. I followed the tradition and took this very serious step in my young life (I never shouted, and that always sort of bothered me, yet I did confess and believed).

I remained in Coldwater and finished high school during the time when the Mississippi schools were still segregated into black schools and white schools. However, things were changing during that time, and soon the schools integrated.

REBELLED AGAINST GOD FOR A SHORT WHILE

I left high school and went to college at Tuskegee Institute/ University in Tuskegee, Alabama. Like most young people just leaving home, I became a little rebellious and decided that I did not believe in God anymore. I remember going back home for college break and talking to my dad about something, and he asked me about going to church. I said a horrible thing to him. I said I didn't believe in God anymore. The room got deathly quiet, and I saw the expression of sorrow on my father's face. I saw the hurt in his eyes so great that it broke my heart and I began to cry. I had hurt the man who had begotten me by saying I didn't believe in my Father anymore. That one scene set me back on the straight path about my belief in God. I knew I still believed.

Don't get me wrong; I did not go back to college and start attending church every Sunday like when I was growing up. No, I am not saying that at all; what I am saying is I let go of the spirit that was telling me there was no God. I rebuked that spirit, and he is long gone. My God is my life, and He has always been with me even when I was straying. He tells us that He will never leave us or forsake us, and I know it to be true. He is the only rock to hold on to.

I MET MY HUSBAND AT TUSKEGEE

While at Tuskegee, I met a young, aspiring veterinary student in college, and he became my husband of over twenty-five years. We had two beautiful daughters from this union, Ericka and Nickole. Fairly early in our marriage, we joined the Seventh Day Adventist church and started keeping the seventh-day Sabbath. We were active in the church for over twenty years and were considered "good SDA Christians." We

FAMILY PORTRAIT - PARENTS AND ALL MY BROTHERS AND SISTERS

My Family from left to right: brother Wally, sister Pam, sister Jurline, brother Elmer, brother Bernard, brother Tyrone, brother Michael, oldest -brother Earl, sister Bobbie, and myself . Father and mother front: Annie Ruth and John Earl Sipp.

went to church every week, and we had many SDA friends and acquaintances. Our first church home was at the Wheaton SDA church, where I was rebaptized by Pastor McGraw. I loved Pastor McGraw; he was a very kind and knowledgeable Caucasian man who nursed us and fed us the manner of the word until we were ready for baptism. Later, we moved our membership to a black congregation in Brinklow, Maryland—the Emmanuel SDA church. This is where we spent many years as part of that congregation. We had many Seventh Day Adventist friends and acquaintances: Henry Fordham, Wintley Phipps, Henry Wright, C. D. Brooks, Larry and Sarah; Warrick and Christine; the Phillips, Sister Wright, and the Neumans, just to mention a few, but there were many others. We were there until our divorce in 2001; then my ex-husband and I went our separate ways.

From about 2002 until 2009, I was sporadically in and out of different church congregations. I prayed but kept God pretty much at arm's length because I was still disoriented and hurting from my divorce. At times, I attended several Sunday churches even though I never let go of the Sabbath as being the true day that God set aside in the beginning. I kept busy in the world and at work; that was what I needed to do to keep going. I bought and sold three houses, I tried to start a business, I learned about solar power, and I dabbled in many other business ventures or projects. I did this because I needed to do something to fill the void in my life left from the divorce; I was trying to fill it. I was not having any success on the dating scene, so I turned to other projects.

MY FAMILY: PARENTS, SIBLINGS,

Sister Jurline, Mom,
sister Bobbie, Me,
sister Pam

Mom (Annie Ruth), Me
and Dad (John Earl Sipp)

My Children, Grand Children, and My Ex-Husband

Ann, Ericka, Michael, Nickole,
Amber, Thomas, Aliyah , Michael, Dani

GOD STARTED DRAWING ME BACK TO HIM

In about 2009, I started feeling the drawing of the Holy Spirit and the urging to get back to the Bible. I started having strange dreams of disasters coming. I felt an overwhelming urge to start reading the Bible again, and I did. I was told by the Spirit to read only the Bible and not Ellen White's writings. I did that, and Yahushua began to open the words of the Bible to my understanding like never before. I started visiting surrounding SDA Churches but found that I was fed more when I prayed and studied at home. I recommitted my life to Christ, and I knew that was where I needed to be.

By 2010, I was totally committed to following Christ wherever He led me. I bought a small piece of land in Tennessee, prepared to leave my home in Maryland, and moved to the hills of Tennessee because I felt that was where the Holy Spirit was leading me. I quit my job, bought that piece of land with an old singlewide house on it, and moved.

At that time, my brother Michael was alive and well and helped me move into the house in 2011, and to clear the land somewhat. However, he did not stay with me because his wife, Toni, was not committed to my plan. In her own words, "I did not buy in to this," I could understand her point because it was my dream and my plan given to me and not to Mike and Toni. I appreciated all the help my brother Mike and Toni provided to me during the setup and transition stage.

Mike and Toni moved backed to Memphis. It was just me and my two small dogs living alone in the hills of Tennessee. But I completely believed in my heart that this was where the Most High wanted me to be.

It was March 11, 2011, when the horrible earthquake hit Japan. This just confirmed to me that the world was falling apart and that this is where I needed to be. Also, everyone was talking about the Mayan 2012 prophecy, and maybe I was also caught up in that frenzy (I did not believe the world was ending, but I believed a terrible disaster would happen and that I needed to be out of the cities).

If I were to give a time when my spiritual awakening first started, I would have to go back to about 2008 or 2009, when I first started having end-time dreams and visions. I did not recognize them as such then; I just felt the spirit on me, speaking to my mind. It was this new spiritual awareness that I could not understand, and in many cases I would question my own thoughts. Was it me, or was it coming from outside of me? Sometimes that can be a difficult question to answer, and only constant seeking in prayer can help to resolve that.

I think it was about late 2008 when I first heard the voice of God audibly. I was in my kitchen, talking to myself about all the crazy things going on in the world, when I heard an audible voice say, "What do you think you have been praying for?" I immediately knew it was the voice of God, and I said, "Wow, it sounds like a black man's voice." I told my sister Jerri about it—that I had heard the voice of God and that He sounds like a black man. We chuckled, and that was the end of it. My sister Jerri is my witness that this did happen.

I purchased my Tennessee property on May 30, 2010, with the intention of moving there by 2011. I planned for my family to come down in March 2011 for spring break (at that point, I was still working in Maryland). I wanted them to see the new homestead location. I purchased the place so that I and my family would have a place to run to in times of trouble. That same weekend is when the Japan earthquake happened (8.9 on the Richter scale) that really shook up the whole world and made me want to expedite my move as soon as possible.

By the summer of 2011, I had quit my job and moved to my small place. I had left a million-dollar home to go into foreclosure and moved to a less-than-poverty-level singlewide trailer house. Of course, all my family thought I had lost my mind at that point. But nobody said much about it; as far as they could see, I was still acting normal, but they just did not agree with my decision to move to the mountains.

CAUGHT UP IN THE 2011 FRENZY- A LOT OF THINGS HAPPENED IN 2011

So 2011 was a very highly spiritual year. I was not the only one being driven to move and do things out of the ordinary. There were many others experiencing the same things. There was a kind of spiritual energy prevalent that we could not explain. Now as I look back on it, I am reminded of the movie *Close Encounters of the Third Kind*. Surely something was getting ready to happen; even Harold Camping had prophesied that the rapture would occur on May 22, 2011. I did not believe that a rapture would happen, but many people had their ascension gowns on and were terribly disappointed.

Tragedy did strike my family. My oldest brother Earl's son Aaron was killed in a horrible construction accident, and we buried him on May 22, 2011. It was in November 2011 when I believe the Most High started giving me revelations on the

Revelation 12 sign in the Bible and showing me how this sign would play out in the end-time scenario. The information I believe He revealed to me pointed to something major that would happen in 2015. I did not know what, but I knew it involved Israel. I was blessed enough to have been able to travel to Israel in 2015.

Also, it was in October 2011 when the Most High revealed to me that I was an Israelite. He revealed to me that I was of the natural seed of Jacob/Israel. That was also the time that my mother was very ill, so I remember that occasion very well. I told all my family members about this revelation. I told them that we are the true Israelites. We are the children of Israel who the Bible speaks of. I told my family that God told me this information Himself, and He did. I have known that I was a true Israelite since October 2011, even though I have been a Sabbath keeper since 1979, when I joined the Seventh Day Adventist Church. It was through the study of the Bible that we were convinced that the seventh-day Sabbath was never changed, and Sunday worship was by decree of the Roman Catholic Church.

THE YEAR 2012 CAME AND WENT

The year 2012 came and went without much notable happening. I was now living in Tennessee alone, just me and my two dogs. My family could not understand this, but they had no choice but to accept it. I was content, and I kept busy with fixing up the place and spending time in prayer and worship.

My daughter Nickole and her husband came over to visit one Sunday. I was showing my son-in-law my mountain land when I slipped and broke my leg. But all ended well; they took me to the hospital, and my leg healed without any problems. In fact, the doctors said it healed like I was seventeen years old (trust me, I am not).

Failed Mayan Prophecy: Many people were disappointed that nothing happened with the 2012 Mayan calendar prediction. However, since I never believed the world was going to end, I just kept studying and praying, trying to get closer to my God. It was at the end of 2012 when I started having many, many dreams; some were downright bothersome, and I did not understand them at all. I recorded them in my journal, but for the most part, I have never shared them with anyone.

This ends my brief autobiographical by-pass to show you who I am. Now we are caught up and back to the year 2013. It was early 2013 when things really began to change for me in a spiritual sense. This brings us back to the point where we left off: my seeing all the spaceships gathered outside of my home.

SPACESHIPS AND LOGOS: SOME GOOD, SOME EVIL

Plan B : Drive down highway. Angels will send high frequency vibrations into vehicle to change molecular configuration, allowing vehicle to be lifted into the Space Craft.

4

THIS IS WHEN THE FIERY TRIALS BEGINS: THE HONEYMOON WAS OVER

I MENTIONED MY experience of seeing numerous lights and spaceships outside and surrounding my home. The first time I saw this was on April 24, 2013. Up until that point and even for several days after that, I was still very happy and peaceful. But one day not long after seeing the lights, I was in worship; I was sitting on the floor, playing music and praising the Father, Yahushua, and the Holy Spirit. I knew Yahushua was there because I could feel His spiritual presence communicating with me. I would tell Him how much I loved Him; He would tell me He loved me more and that I could never love Him more than He loved me. He said He loves me with godly love and that my human love could never compare to His love. I understood that, and it sat well with my soul.

However, that day things went a little differently than normal. During worship, He told me to look out my window. I did as he instructed, and sure enough I saw all the spaceships blinking like they were listening to everything that was going on in my house. That is the knowing I got from the Spirit. They were watching and listening to me; they knew and saw every word said and action done by me.

Then Yahushua told me to look around the room. I did, and I saw all over my walls what looked like thin, electronic light sensors emanating out of the walls. They bore the same logos I saw on the ships outside of my window, and they were blinking. Then He told me that I must rebuke them because they are from Satan's ships. He taught me how to rebuke them, and when I did, their lights went out, so they left. This was very frightening because these are the lights that I had been seeing for a couple of months, and I thought it was all good.

Yahushua also pointed me to a certain sensor in the corner of the room and told me to rebuke him; He said it was Satan himself. I started to rebuke him, but he would not go away; he only moved above me and was just staring at me. I could sense that he might have been in some spaceship sitting outside and was just looking at me. Needless to say, this is where my trouble began. From that point on, my world was turned upside down. They are here—the fallen angels/aliens are already with us. I can see them. They can communicate with me telepathically. I can communicate with them telepathically. They were everywhere. They were in my bathroom; they watched me shower and made faces and drew pictures of my body parts. They tried to give me a different gospel as to who they were and where they came from. They had invaded my home; they were alien invaders/fallen angels in my home. I was told by Christ not to talk to them, yet they were constantly showing me things that I had never seen before that captured my attention.

For example, they can cause matter to change right before your eyes. They could do things like drawing pictures on the floor that told a story, while they telepathically told me what they were drawing. I remember once when they were doing that, and Christ or my angel sent Teco over and made him sit right on the picture to get my attention. I was totally captured by what I was seeing in real time. I was reminded not to talk to them or engage in what they were doing. This was very hard to do because I never knew where the messages or impressions were coming from. I was not always able to distinguish good angels from bad ones.

It was during this time that I was told the aliens were scanning my house to determine my DNA abduction suitability. I was told to keep Teco near me because when they scanned and found canine DNA, they would not want my DNA. I got the impression that the grey aliens who were on the ground worked with the aliens in the spacecraft to scout out candidates for abduction.

One evening, I was very tired from the day's activities but was instructed not to lie down or go to sleep; they were scanning my house. I sat on the couch all night trying to stay awake. Teco was told to lie beside my feet. At about 2:00 a.m., I started hearing a very loud buzzing or humming sound, and a yellow light appeared on my ceiling. I do not know if I had fallen asleep; I don't think so, but at that time I saw them plainly looking through my window. I saw the grey aliens, and they looked like the pictures we have all seen with the big heads and big eyes. They did not try to come inside but were just peering through my window. It was very frightening. The next day, Teco took me to the spot where they were standing, and I could see evidence that they had been there—not only the night before, but it appeared that they had been doing that many times. I was able to see markings on the ground; they always leave evidence such as their call sign markings. These markings are not evident to the natural eyes but since the Most High had given me spiritual eyes during this time, I could see the call sign markings on the ground which let me know they had been there multiple times. This was the evidence which Teco led me to.

**Grey Aliens Peeping in Window.
Not all Greys look exactly alike,
but all had big heads and eyes.**

THE LIGHT SENSORS ON THE WALLS: SOME GOOD SOME BAD

I was shown that there were sensors from the holy angels in the room also. I needed to rebuke the evil angels, or they would seek out and destroy the sensors of the Holy angels. When that happened, the good angels would not be able to hear me. I was rebuking over and over until I was totally worn out. Yet I was never able to tell if I was spending time rebuking the good as well as the bad ones. It wore me out. One day, I was so frustrated that I asked Yahushua to please show me the good angels, and to my surprise there were very many good angels' sensors around. He showed this to me by having the good angels light up, and a circle of light was drawn around them; the circle indicated the good angels. This gave my heart comfort and encouragement. I was doing it right.

THE SPIDER ROBOT—A SENSOR KILLER

I was shown a small, spiderlike sensor robot, which the enemy used to crawl around and destroy the sensors of the holy angels. By destroying these sensors, the bad angels assured that the holy angels would not be able to hear me. I knew this spider-sensor killer was destroying many good sensors because I was told this was happening. I became so tired and worn out that I could not think straight. These invaders in my home had the ability to send the spirit of sleep on me anytime they wanted to, yet I was told not to go to sleep during the day because they were the ones causing me to feel sleepy. Normally, I do not sleep during the day, but it was becoming almost impossible for me to fight off the sleep spirit because of fatigue.

I also became afraid to go to sleep at night; I felt this was when they really attacked me. I would wake up seeing all types

**Similar to the spacecraft
I saw in the skies**

**Similar to sensors on my walls –
but clear light not in color**

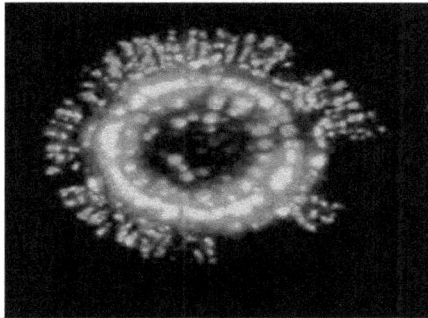

of animals on my wall and ceiling. I would see what looked like operating-room equipment coming out of my ceiling. I would see beings of all types move in and out of my home. I was being spiritually attacked daily. I would wake up rebuking entities that I heard and saw in my room. They knew my thoughts, so I was told to be careful of what I focused my mind on. They can send messages telepathically and also read our thoughts. This interfered with my mind because I began to feel like I could not pray without them intruding in my thoughts even though I was assured it was OK.

Here is an example of when the killer sensor attacked. One time I knew the killer spider sensor had destroyed all but one or two of the good sensors. I was told not to look at the remaining sensors because the enemies would perceive where they were based on my attention toward them; they were watching me. One day, I was really feeling afraid, so I wrote a note and looked over to where the sensor was to get a response. But to my horror and surprise, they had found the sensor and wrote a profane message on my Ten Commandment plaque on the wall. It was a very filthy, sexual message written over the Ten Commandments. The sensor had been positioned on the plaque. I was devastated to know that they had destroyed that sensor and were mocking me by defaming my Ten Commandments.

The attacks were not all just mental. I was being attacked to the point that physical marks were being left on my body in the form of bruises, scratches, and swellings. These marks would be on my arms, thighs, butt, and face.

I was afraid to go to sleep. They controlled my dogs and made me think my clothes were contaminated. They would cause Teco to bark at me to make me take off certain items of clothing. Teco could see the entities, and I knew he could because I could see what he was seeing. They tried to make me go naked by convincing me that there was something on my clothes. (That reminded me of all the cases where demon-possessed people were found running naked in the streets.) I refused to strip and rebuked the dog. Of course, I was afraid and wondered what I had done to cause all these attacks from the enemy. The attacks were very difficult.

When they wrote the horrible message on the Ten Commandments plaque, it really frightened me. I told Yahushua that I was afraid and wanted to leave. He told me not to leave and that He would call for backup help, but it would take about three days before help arrived. Of course, I said, "What? Three days? There is no way I will stay here for three days." He told me not to be afraid, but at that point I was totally afraid. I had made up my mind that I was not going to stay in that house for three days until help arrived (it was a test). I was determined to leave and go somewhere. Did I lose my faith there? As I look back, I think I did, but it was all I knew to do at that time.

I grabbed my dogs and decided that I was going to go into town and stay at a hotel. That probably turned out to be one of the worst nights of my life. I was trying to run from these demonic attacks, and I ran, but it did not accomplish anything. The situation got worse.

I Ran because I Was Afraid

I went into town and got a room at a little hotel on the strip. But lo and behold, when I got there, the bad angels were already there. The sensors were on the room walls everywhere I looked. I felt defeated. Satan told me, "You cannot run from me." I was told by the good angels that the aliens were trying to abduct me and that they would probably try it while I was at the hotel. However, like before, if they scanned the room and did not find acceptable DNA, they would not try to take me. The voice that

I was hearing said to always keep Teco close to my feet so that when they scanned for me, they would pick up canine DNA and would not want to abduct me.

THE ANGELS TOLD ME THE RESCUE PLAN – PLAN A

When I got to the hotel room, I was told that the angels would rescue me. But first the good angels had to destroy the sensors of the enemy that were in the room. Then I could escape, and the enemy would not be able to follow me. The good angels were going to pick me up and take me to safety before the evil ones got to me. This seemed reasonable, and I needed all the help I could get.

The good angels telepathically laid out the plan. They showed me a diagram of what I needed to do. Suddenly, the TV reception in my room was interrupted, and the plan was displayed on the TV.

FOLLOWING THE PLAN

The first part of their plan was to destroy the sensors of the evil ones, cutting off their communication. These sensors were located on the walls. The good angels accomplished this by running something through the air conditioner that started drying up or killing the sensors. I heard the air conditioner kick on, and a very strange-sounding generator began to run.

I was not allowed to leave the room or open the door. When the air conditioner and generator sound began, I noticed the sensors on the wall drying up and falling off like living creatures.

I was told that once this started happening, the enemies would begin to scan the room. They wanted to see what was happening because their communication was being corrupted. Sure enough, around that same time, I sensed the room being scanned. A familiar yellow glow appeared on the ceiling, and then Teco came over and lay on my feet. I was instructed to go stand in the corner, close to the air conditioner, by the window. As I did, again Teco came and lay on my feet while I was standing. I never called him or indicated in any way that he should do that. He was being totally controlled by someone other than me.

After the enemy began to scan the room, a grey alien came into the room. It didn't come through the door but rather slithered under it like smoke or an energy-wave form. It looked like a grey alien but did not seem to have the physical form that we are accustomed to. I did not see Yahushua in the room, but I knew He was there. He grabbed the alien form before it could get to us and started to feed it into the sucking air-condition unit. I watched as this thing struggled against being pulled into that vent. It was scary. After it was over, I asked Yahushua, "What was that?" He told me it was a "buddy" of one of the air battle casualties—the battle I had participated in earlier. They were coming to get me. During this entire experience, I stood erect for over three hours with Teco remaining at my feet, never leaving. After about three hours of the air conditioner running, all the sensors had dried up and fallen from the walls.

They lay around the border of the wall like dead roaches. They were once light beings but now appeared as dead bugs on the floor. It was time to leave, but I was told that I could not take my truck. The enemy had placed active sensors in my truck and would be able to spot me immediately. I had to leave on foot.

The plan was for me and the dogs to leave the hotel with nothing but my purse. I was to walk up the street, where they would signal me and tell me where to meet them. This was so they could pick me up; since the enemy sensors had been destroyed, they would not be able to track and locate me. That was the plan.

Both Princess and Teco were with me at the hotel. Teco was obedient, but when we walked out the door, Princess started acting like she was afraid of me and began to run. I left home in such a hurry that I didn't bring my dog leashes, so they had to walk loose. I saw a dollar store and attempted to buy the leashes, but they would not let me in because they were closing (it must have been about 9:00 p.m.). I went back and called the dogs to follow me, but they ignored me and started running in circles. Then they took off and ran to where I could not see them at all.

They had run away from the meeting area, where we were supposed to be picked up. I had been told to follow Teco, but now Teco was following Princess, and both were acting strangely. It was as if they were being led in circles by something other than themselves. They were. I was told to remember the call sign and to walk to the spot, look for the call sign on the ground, and wait there to be picked up.

The dogs ran off, so I decided to proceed to the spot without them. I thought that maybe Teco knew where the spot was and would be there waiting for me. I went to where I thought the spot would be based on my understanding of the plan, but it was not there (I looked for the call sign on the ground). I was told not to look up because the enemy would be able to spot me from above by my "glowing" eyes. So I avoided looking up to see which spaceships were over me, but I did see many spaceships in the distance just by looking at the horizon.

I was told to go to another location. I am not sure if I received this information later telepathically or if it was in the original plan and I just missed it. I started walking up behind a big warehouse store (I think it was Walmart), and I saw a call sign on the ground. I was happy, but then I looked closely and realized that it was the wrong ship's call sign. I kept walking, hoping I would run across the right one nearby. The spot that I came to had a call sign. It looked like a tattoo that had been burned into the ground, but it did not match the pattern of the one I was looking for.

I kept walking and saw what looked like a police officer or security guard. He asked what I was doing out and around that area that late. I told him that my dogs had run off and that I thought they might have come up that way. He said he had not seen them and that it was best that I hurry out of that area. At that point, my frustration level was very high, and I decided to go back to the hotel for the night. I was afraid to look up, and I had walked probably two or three miles looking for the call sign and my dogs. I was exhausted and ready to give up, and I just wanted to go back to the hotel. Then I remembered that when I left the room, I had left the key, so the door was locked.

By that time, it was after midnight. When I got back to the hotel, the lobby was closed, and nobody answered the bell. I waited for at least thirty minutes, but nobody was available to let me back into my room. There I was, locked out of my hotel room. My dogs had run off, and I was tired, scared, and alone. I went to my truck, prayed, cried, and asked the Lord what I had done to deserve this. I was broken. I cried myself to sleep and slept for a couple of hours in my truck outside the hotel building. Oh, what a night!

Around daybreak, I heard dogs yelping. I looked, and coming from around the building were my dogs. I didn't know where they had been, but I was glad to see them. Shortly after that, I heard a voice speaking to me in the truck. I was told that the enemy had missed a couple of the good angels' strategically hidden sensors, and that is how they were able to contact me. They gave me a new plan, which involved them lifting the whole truck up and taking me and the truck into the spaceship. During this conversation, there seemed to be at least three personalities present; I just got that feeling. They were speaking, and I noticed that one had a woman's voice. The female voice surprised me, and when she finished talking, I asked, "Who are you?" It was as if they expected me to ask that question. She replied, "I am the Mother of the Night Sky." She continued giving me information as if she was always present. I will always remember that moment because her voice caught me off guard. Since that night, I have heard a female voice speak to me several times in different situations.

The new plan involved them sending certain sound frequencies into my truck. Once it reached a certain frequency, it would change the truck's molecular structure. When a certain level was reached, I was to start driving down this road. This would make the truck able to be lifted into the spaceship. I asked how I would know when to start driving and was told that Teco's ears had been tuned. When he started to howl, I needed to start driving. However, right after our conversation, I had a vision where I saw something burrowing into Teco's ears. It frightened me because it showed his ears being destroyed. Had Satan intercepted the plan?

We sat there for quite a while. I could sense that I was hearing very high-pitched noises, but Teco never reacted like they said he would, so I never left. We sat so long in the hotel parking lot that the clerk came out and told us that we had to leave because I was loitering.

THE NEW PLAN—PLAN B

After I was kicked out of the hotel parking lot, I went to the Walmart parking lot because I knew how to find it. Remember that I had just moved into the area, so this town was not familiar to me. I did not want to go back to my house because I was still afraid of what was there. I was also still hearing a very high frequency sound in my ears, although I wasn't hearing any more communications from Yahushua or the angels. I looked for sensors in the truck to see if I could hear from someone, but there was nothing. I didn't know what to do, so I just sat in the parking lot for a while.

My dogs had not eaten for two days (neither had I), so I went into Walmart to get food and water for them. I bought some fruit for myself and some disposable bowls, and then I fed them and gave them water. While still in the parking lot, I looked up into the sky. I saw a vision of the new plan shown in the sky, illustrated in the clouds. I saw a car on a road. The clouds formed another road, lifting the car onto the new road that was going up into the sky. This cloud formation was unmistakably the new plan. I knew it meant that I needed to follow the plan.

After the dogs had finished eating, I walked them to do their business and returned to my truck. I still had not heard from anyone (no voices), and the only thing that I had seen was the vision in the clouds of the new plan. I knew it was time to get on the road. It was time to implement plan B. I left Walmart and headed down the highway in the direction I understood I was to go. At that point, I was still hearing the high frequency sounds in my ears, and the sound seemed to be getting louder and louder as I traveled. Teco was standing up in the back and also pacing back and forth from one side to the other. Princess was also acting very restless. I took this as a sign that something was happening.

I continued driving and found myself going deeper and deeper into the rural areas. Then I was headed up a mountain. The dogs were restless, but I did not see any evidence of the call sign that I was to look for. I drove and drove until the road I was on was headed toward a mountain. Suddenly my heart sank. Directly above this mountain were several clouds whose shapes formed the faces and bodies of dozens of grey aliens. This was their mountain, and they were drawing me there. When I realized what was going on, I immediately pulled off the road to turn around. My heart was racing. They were trying to abduct me, and I was driving myself right to their headquarters.

I turned around and started speeding away from the mountain. That is when I started seeing call signs, but it was the call sign of the enemy. They knew I had discovered what they were doing, and now they were after me. Their call signs started appearing on the road in front of me, very illuminated. The spaceships were after me, and they were going to abduct my truck. I panicked. I was driving as fast as I could down that country road. When I would see the call signs in the road, I would swerve my truck to keep from driving over the logo. I knew that for aliens to take my truck, they would have to get a lock on the truck for several seconds. I would drive, see the sign in the road, and then swerve. This was going on for miles as I was rushing to get away. People were pulling off the road as I approached them; I was driving like a deranged lunatic. I was afraid. I was praying out loud, saying, "Help me, Lord. They are trying to abduct me. What do I do?" Repeatedly I was praying, "What do I do?" Then I heard in my spirit, "Go back to Walmart." I did; it was the only place I knew to go.

When I got back to Walmart, I felt relieved. I sat in the parking lot and prayed while trying to compose myself. I was in tears and wondering again why this was happening to me. "Lord, what am I doing wrong in your sight? I am doubting myself. I am clearly not doing something right. I am trying to be obedient, but it sure looks (and feels) like I am missing the mark." I remembered that in the past, I had been in the Walmart store, and Yahushua would talk to me there. Since I was not hearing from Him in my truck, I thought maybe I could get a connection in Walmart.

I went in and started praying, "Lord, can you hear me?" I was in tears but trying not to draw attention to myself. I said again, "Lord, can you hear me?" In my ear, I heard what sounded like a microphone click open like when you establish contact with a two-way radio. I knew the channel was open, but He did not say a word. I remember saying, "If you can't talk, just make a click again to let me know that you hear me." He made the click again just like I asked, and I was comforted. This was another test. He let me know later that He could always hear me when I was in my truck.

I left Walmart that day and returned to my house to face my demons. I learned I would rather face my demons at home than to be abducted by fallen angels. However, it was not over yet. There was much more to come.

I was headed toward a mountain and above the mountain as cloud formations , I saw dozens of Greys Watching me.

5

FORCED TO GO BACK HOME TO FACE MY DEMONS

WHEN I FINALLY got back home, the demons were very angry at me for leaving and thinking I could get away from them. Remember, they were already waiting for me when I arrived at the hotel. I was in my bedroom and heard a loud crash that severely frightened me. They had caused my pots to fall from my ceiling, creating a loud, scary crash. They let me know they were not happy with my leaving.

I was back home now, and still I was seeing all kinds of things that frightened me. Princess was still running from me, acting like she was afraid to come near me; Teco was still attacking her and making her stay away from me. He stayed close to me and seemed to be protecting me. It was obvious that he was being controlled by some power outside of me. I knew that it was Yahushua who was protecting me. Also at night, Princess would start barking as if something had entered the house, so I knew she was also seeing things she did not understand, and it frightened her. Princess has always been an alarmist and reacted openly to things that were out of the ordinary for her. Keep in mind that I could look at myself in the mirror and see that my eyes were glowing; Princess saw it too, so I understood why she was afraid.

MORE OF THE SAME ATTACKS IN THE DAYS THAT FOLLOWED

During the next several days, things escalated both day and night. I was constantly seeing demonic entities, both on the inside and on the outside. I was instructed to rebuke them. There is no doubt in my mind that I was told to rebuke them openly. I was praying every day to be delivered from these apparitions and manifestations. The response was that I needed to rebuke them both on the inside and on the outside in the sky. I was commanded to do battle with the enemy.

During the day, I would go outside, look up into the sky, and see the spaceships. At times, I would see scores of them hovering over and around my house. I would see battles in the sky between the good angels and the evil angels. My job was to assist the good angels by looking at the ships, which would automatically cause them to reveal who they were. If they were the enemy, I would lock my laser-eye vision on to them, and this would allow the good angels to shoot down the evil craft. I watched this happen many times repeatedly. I could see laser beams come out from the good angels' ships and destroy the ships that I had locked my vision on; they were the evil angels. There were both jet fighters and circular spacecraft involved in these battles. This went on for days when I was outside looking up into the sky, rebuking the demons and using my laser vision to point out the enemy. This part was exciting because I felt that I was participating in the battle.

TECO USED AS A SPIRIT-GUIDE DOG TO SHOW ME EVIDENCE OF FALLEN ANGELS

While I was not in battle with the space entities, I was being shown how the fallen angels are present all around us and can be seen by those who have eyes to see. Yes, I had been given eyes to see them. Many of them look just like the small grey aliens you see in pictures. This is a true depiction of what many of them look like. Teco had been given eyes to see also; he was given to me as a confirmation to prove that all of this was not just in my mind.

I was told to walk Teco on a leash and that he would show me the evidence of the fallen angels. I did as I was instructed, and I was horrified at what I found out. They are everywhere, and the evidence of them is everywhere—in the rocks, on the trees, and in the open fields. I could hardly walk twenty feet before seeing evidence of their presence. I walked Teco on leash, and he would act like a hunting dog. When he found some-thing that he wanted me to see, he would stop and look back at me to indicate that I should look. I did, and I would always see things—faces on rocks and trees or things put in patterns and configurations to let me know that the fallen angels had been there. First we went around my house, and I saw evidences of things I had never seen before. Then we went out by the road near the horse pen, Teco leading and me just following and being amazed at the things I was seeing.

6

MY DAUGHTER'S SURPRISE VISIT—THE SPARK THAT LIT THE FIRE

ON THE DAY after the hotel adventure, I received a surprise visit from my daughter Ericka. Ericka had come over unannounced, and I was pleasantly surprised to see her. Before this visit, she had been very angry at me because of something I said when she was last at my house. We had been having a conversation, and she was going on about her friend Toni and made the comment that Toni was so vain. I then said that she was vain also. That made her very angry, and because of that, she had cut me off and was not going to talk to me anymore, and she didn't.

I had been trying to reopen communication with her by sending her messages and videos that I found interesting; I had no bad feelings toward her at all and really was surprised that she reacted to my statement as strongly as she did. I never intended to offend her; she and Toni were good friends and had a lot in common, so I thought she knew that birds of a feather flocked together (I guess not). So when she turned up unannounced at my house and Teco and Princess were not getting along at all, I saw this as an opportunity to have her take Princess away. Remember, I was under severe stress; Teco was constantly biting at Princess, not allowing her to get near me as if she was a threat to me. In hindsight, maybe my thinking was skewed and what I asked her to do was somewhat over the top. But the way I was seeing it, Princess was still running from me. I felt that maybe the evil ones had put some kind of tracker on her and were trying to use her against me. So when Ericka showed up, I saw this as a good opportunity to send Princess away with her.

When Ericka got to my house, I told her about all the demonic manifestations I had been seeing and explained to her how Teco was attacking Princess; she even saw his actions herself, but she did not understand all the other things that had been going on. Even when Ericka entered my area and was still outside, I could see that she was being marked with what I call tracking devices. I could see them on her body just like I saw them in the sky. I tried to show her some of the things I was seeing, but of course she saw nothing and probably thought I had lost my mind.

I then explained to her that I thought that maybe Princess had some kind of tracking chip in her body and that she had been programmed and was being controlled by aliens. I explained to her how Princess was behaving and how Teco was acting and that I needed her to take Princess for me. I said I didn't advise her to keep Princess in their house because the aliens would track her to Ericka's house and attack the family; therefore, she should take her to the dog pound. I know that sounds harsh, but that was my thinking after being attacked. I did not want her and my granddaughter Amber to be subjected to these attacks also. The attacks had been going on with me for almost a month, and by that time my only focus was to stop the demonic attacks any way I could. I was willing to get rid of anything that might have been a source of the attacks. I felt that Princess was a conduit for the demons, and so I was attempting to remove her. This might have been the thing that caused Ericka to completely lose it; she is a dog lover.

Ericka agreed to take Princess away, and she did. Little did I know that she went back and told the whole family that I had totally lost my mind. Even though I had not been talking to Ericka because of our disagreement over vanity, Nickole and I still talked often, and I had even told her about some of the experiences I had been having and the fact that I had been seeing things.

Princess had been gone for about two or three days, and I was out walking Teco near the horse pen. When I looked up, there were my ex-husband, Michael, and Ericka driving up. I was surprised to see them, but I was happy to see them and greeted them with a smile and a "good to see you." They pulled into my driveway, and Mike gave me a polite cursory hug and greeting. Ericka said that they were just going over to meet my neighbor. Ericka had already met my neighbor, so she knew and had talked to Teresa before; I assumed she just wanted her dad to see and meet her mother's neighbors. I only thought good of that; I had no idea what she was doing, but Yahushua knew exactly what she was up to. They left and went up to see Teresa, and I finished walking Teco and went back into my house. Shortly after that, I saw Ericka and my ex-husband leave my neighbor's house. I assumed they had met and that all was well.

On Friday, May 24, 2013, my community experienced a blackout. All lights in the neighborhood went out. I went to my neighbor Teresa's house to find out what had happened. Teresa's husband was a local pastor, so they always knew what was going on in the neighborhood. She informed me that a transformer had blown out, and the officials said that there was no telling when it would be fixed. That alarmed me, so I called Nickole to tell her that my lights were out, that my truck was also having electrical problems (it was), and that I might need to call on her. She and Danny offered to come over and stay with me if the lights didn't come back on. I was afraid to be in my house with all the attacks when it was pitch black, and fear started to set in again.

I remembered that the phone system was on a different electrical current than the house, so I pulled out my old manual phone and plugged it in; it worked. It had gotten dark, especially in my rural area. Then out of the blue, my brother Mike called and talked to me awhile; that gave me comfort. While I was on the phone, Nickole had been trying to call to tell me that they were coming over if I needed them. Nickole had already told me that she and her husband would stay the night with me since I was afraid, and I agree because I was really afraid by then.

However, something happened (some demonic attack occurred), and my fear level shot sky high. I think I thought the aliens would try to abduct me during the power outage, so I panicked. Nickole called back and told me that they were on their way. That is when I told her, almost in panic mode, "I don't want to stay here tonight. I am not staying here another night. Do not even come into this place. I will come out, and you can take me back to your house." When they got to my house, I rushed out to their truck immediately. I took no clothes or supplies, only my purse and Teco.

Little did I know what was going on in the background. Ericka and my ex-husband had called everyone in my family and told them that I had lost my mind and that he and the police were going to pick me up and commit me to a mental hospital on the following day, which would have been Saturday, May 25, 2013.

I know that Yahushua caused the transformer to blow and made me afraid the night before their plan was to be executed. I believe this was in order to get me away from the house so that when they planned to pick me up, I would not be there. I believe that is why I went to Nickole's house so readily, and it was a last-minute decision to leave. This was Yahushua's doing to foil their evil plan against me.

MY FAMILY WAS PLANNING TO HAVE ME COMMITTED

I had no idea what Ericka and Michael were planning. I didn't know that any of this wickedness was being planned in the background. Michael had told my sister Jurline (Jerri) that he was going to have me committed. How could he do this? We had been divorced for over fifteen years, and he knew nothing about how I lived my life. I found out that it was because of my daughter Ericka; she was behind all of it. My daughter had become my enemy, and it had begun with her picking up Princess. Remember, Ericka had no knowledge of what had happened at the hotel. Her only contact with me was when she came over and picked up Princess.

Nickole and Danny picked me up and took me to their house on Friday night, May 24, 2013. They too, had been contacted and knew what was being discussed in the background. From later conversations, I heard that my ex-husband had tried to get Danny to be involved in the police raid, but Danny was not up for that. I am not exactly sure how this next part happened, but I think Nickole called Jurline and told her that they had me at their house. Then my sister Jurline, my sister Bobbie, and Bobbie's husband, Jessie, left Memphis very early and headed to Nickole's house to get me before my ex-husband and Ericka had me committed to a mental hospital. Again, I was totally oblivious to any of this, and since I didn't know that Danny was being told that I was crazy, I wondered why he kept coming into my room to check on me like I was a child when I was at their house. I also noticed that my granddaughter Dani was not at home. I found out later that my ex-husband's wife had told them to remove the child because she was in danger by being around me. They made her stay with my ex-husband that night for her safety.

MY FAMILY ARRIVES FROM MEMPHIS
When Jurline, Bobbie, and Jessie arrived, they immediately came to my room. I did not know that they were coming until about twenty minutes before they arrived. At that point, I was saying, "What in the world is going on? Why is my family coming here?" Well, I found out when they got there.

After sitting and talking for a short time—the family asking me a few questions and me responding as to what had been going on—I was told that I either had to go back to Memphis with them or be committed to a mental hospital. When I heard this, I was confused and in disbelief.

Jerri said that my ex-husband had told her that he and Ericka were planning to have me committed, and she begged him not to and to allow her to take care of me. Mike reluctantly agreed but said that I had to leave with them that day and not go back to my house. I was shocked and almost speechless (another test?). But somehow I knew that Yahushua had everything under control, and so I agreed to go with them even though I had no decent clothes, no supplies, or anything, but I could not go back to my house. When I had left home the night before, I was wearing bed clothes. Nickole supplied me with some street clothes, even down to underwear, and that is how I left Knoxville, Tennessee.

I was amazed at what was happening to me—and by my own family. And so on May 25, 2013, I left all my belongings and went to Memphis without a hint to my neighbors about what was going on. As far as my neighbors knew (from my ex-husband and Ericka), I was in a mental institution.

7

MY UNEXPECTED MOVE TO MEMPHIS

I LEFT NICKOLE house with my family and went to stay with my sister Jurline, who lives in Memphis in a house that she and I bought together. It is like my second home, but she and her family are the primary residents. Jerri is my older sister, and we have always been very close. Even in childhood, we did everything together. Our religious beliefs are almost the same, so I had no problems staying with her for a while. If anyone knew me, Jerri did.

I moved in and got comfortable. I left Knoxville with nothing—no clothes, no supplies, nothing—but Jerri took care of me with what she owned. In fact, I ended up with more stuff to wear than I owned at home. I did not need anything.

While in Memphis, I was still having dreams and visions, still seeing the same things in the sky, and still being told to rebuke the evil ones. In fact, Satan visited me several times in Memphis. Once he appeared to me, and I felt he was directly in my face, nose to nose. He said to me again, "You cannot run from me." That was a very troubling experience. This happened the same night I arrived in Memphis. So nothing had changed for me in the spirit realm even though I had relocated physically. Nothing had changed because as I established earlier, these demonic spirits are everywhere, and since my eyes had been opened to be able to see into the spirit realm, I could still see them. My only defense was to rebuke them in the name of Yahushua (Jesus Christ), which is the highest name above all demons and principalities.

I was still being told to keep Teco always near me. This created a bit of a problem because no one could understand how and why that dog had to always be with me. Even Pam, my youngest sister, said, "Ann, I remember when you used to rule over your dogs; now you let your dog rule over you. What is wrong with you?" They just didn't know, and if I tried to explain it to them, they would never understand. This was my test, my cross to carry. Yes, in Memphis, I was seeing things that no one else could see. I could determine the spirits of people because Yahushua would give me revelations on them.

Many family members came around to see me and to check me out to see how "crazy Ann" was behaving. My sister even had her pastor to come over to visit and bless the house. I met him but did not spend much time with him because I was advised not to, and to confirm that, Teco reacted to him very hostilely.

When visitors came to see me, most saw that I was still the same person they remembered from before, other than my strange attachment to my dog. I kept telling them that what I was experiencing was because of the supernatural gift given to me by God. Even Jerri asked, "How can it be a gift when you are always seeing demons?" I do not remember what I said, but I believe that my God is training me to do work for His kingdom. That is the faith I had to hold on to. I knew He was with me all the time and was allowing these things to happen to me, so He must have had a reason for it even though it was very difficult for me to understand at times.

I was able to see into the spirit realm, and I could see things that have always been there but were invisible with our normal range of vision. The fact that I was in Memphis did not change what was happening to me in the spirit realm. The visitations continued at night, and I was still being told by Yahushua to rebuke them. This caused a bit of a problem because no one else saw what I saw, and they only heard me rebuking these entities (invisible to them). But Yah is wonderful because there was another person who saw them and kept pointing them out: a little child who was my sister's granddaughter. No one could deny that the child was seeing something, and she and I bonded magnificently.

MY BROTHER MIKE GAVE ME SOME GOOD ADVICE SENT FROM YAHUSHUA

My brother Michael, who also lived in Memphis, came to visit me shortly after I arrived at Jerri's house. Mike and I had been in constant communication during the time that I was having these visitations and experiences. He would call me often, and we would talk for hours about Yahushua, our God and Savior.

Mike was being used by Yahushua to encourage me, and I was encouraging him also. We would talk and pray and have Bible studies on the phone. I shared with him many of the dreams that I was having and some things that Yahushua had revealed to me. I remember once sharing a revelation that Yahushua had shared with me concerning praise, worship, and feelings; Mike blushed and said, "I don't want to hear about that," and I just laughed.

In fact, Mike was the only one I could talk to concerning what was happening to me; he was also being moved by the spirit of God and understood me and the Spirit. Yahushua would give him messages to deliver to me, and I recognize that as so. This was the time during Mike's illness; he was going to the cancer clinic weekly and would often call me on the day of his visit for prayer, and we would talk.

Jurline, Bobbie, and Jessie did not know that Mike and I were always talking to each other, so Mike knew that I was not crazy. My ex-husband was the one who contacted Jerri and told them all types of lies that he made up or had gotten from Ericka. My ex-husband even told Jerri that I had always suffered from schizophrenia in the past. That was a flat-out lie; I have never taken any medicine or suffered from any diseases of that type in the past or ever. I said to Jerri, "You have known me all my life, and we have always discussed everything. When do you remember me having schizophrenia?" She only hung her head and said, "You are right, Ann. Never." Remember, this is my oldest sister, with whom I have shared everything, even to the point of us owning a home together. If anyone knew of any illnesses like that, she would have known. But Jerri was still having trouble with me seeing things. I remember trying to explain to her what I was seeing. I even drew her pictures of the type of space crafts I saw. The space crafts with six windows or portals on them. But she too felt that I was, "seeing things," and did not want me to talk about them or anything else like that.

The Good Advice from a Brother

My brother Mike knew that I was not crazy, and when he came over to see me, that was confirmed in his mind. He gave me some very good advice that I adhere to today. He said, "You can't tell everything to everybody because everybody cannot hear everything." I understood exactly what he meant. The things I was seeing and hearing could not be understood by my family or other people. Generally speaking, if someone is doing things that are not in line with what others expect or what everyone else is doing or saying, that person is labeled crazy by those who cannot understand it. From that point on, I stopped telling everyone about the things I was seeing; even though I still saw many things, I stopped mentioning them to people.

Warning Dream from Yahushua about My Ex-Husband

It was around March 2013 when Yahushua gave me a dream about Michael (my ex-husband), and he was destroying my things. I did not understand the dream at that time, but it became clearer later what the dream meant.

In the dream, I was in my bedroom, and I had fixed everything up so nicely. I had hung curtains, made the bed, and organized the books to be neat and in place. I was very pleased, and I thought that my ex-husband would be pleased also. I called him into the room to show him what I had done. He came into the room and just started tearing everything down and destroying everything I had made. I was so hurt and started crying and saying, "Why are you doing this? Why are you destroying my things?" Then I heard a voice in my dream say, "He was never any good." The dream ended. (I received this dream shortly before he and Ericka tried to have me committed. So you can see why I said I can understand the dream now.)

Yahushua HaMashiach Is From the Tribe Of Judah; The Bible Describes Him as having Feet like Brass Burned In The Fire: Revelation 1:15.

TECO THE SPIRITUAL GUIDE DOG SHOWS EVIDENCE OF FALLEN ANGELS IN MEMPHIS

While in Memphis, I was still able to see many supernatural places where the fallen angels had been. I was shown places where they picked up or maybe abducted people. I could see and recognize the places by the familiar call signs or logos they left.

Just like airports and airplane carriers have certain areas they service that may be different in different cities, so do the angel space crafts. There was a separate group of call signs in Memphis for those spaceships that had that jurisdiction. But there were a few that I recognized from my area, which probably were the higher-level angels or demons. I was told to search out certain ones; again, some were good, and others were on the side of the enemy. Also, I was shown how these vehicles can transform to look like normal planes, weather balloons, or other flying entities that we are accustomed to seeing.

My sister lives near an airport, where planes are constantly taking off and landing. I could see how the spaceships moved out of the way when a plane was headed toward them and moved back to their positions when the airplane passed by. I watched this activity happen numerous times. They were all around the airport, and the air traffic controllers never saw them on their radar. That is how they can be in our skies by the thousands, and we never know it unless they decide to make themselves visible to us.

The space crafts travel on circuits or highways in the skies. Things are very organized. I could see these circuits in the sky, and I call them circuits because the highways reminded me of electrical currents running through the sky. I noticed that all the homes were connected to at least one of these spaceship high-ways that traveled over it. This means that every human is being tracked by angels, some good and some bad. As I observed this, I was reminded of the Bible when it talks about the mark of the beast. The angels' technology for tracking is so far advanced to what we can imagine that the concept of the mark of the beast sounds primitive to me.

As I said, every human is tracked by the angels. They mark us with their particular call signs or logos. I saw these logos on peo-ple. Most were located right on their foreheads just like the Bible describes it. Normally we cannot see these markings, but I was allowed to see them clearly, and on some people I saw, I recognized the fallen angels' call signs. Others I saw had the good angels' call signs on them. It appears that everyone has already been chosen, or their actions have already made the choice for them. That's in the spirit realm, and the physical world will follow.

Teco on the Hunt

One day I was out walking with Teco, and he had taken me to a place where the fallen angels had a call-sign site on the ground. Teco became excited and beckoned me to look. Sure enough, I recognized it to be one. He then went into hunt mode like he was on the track of something and wanted me to follow him. I did, and he quickly took me to another site, and there too, was the sign. He took off again and started toward the woods. I was thinking that he was following more than just a site, and I decided that I was not going any further. I called him back, but he refused to come. Instead, he was trying to get me to follow him. I became nervous about what was in the woods, about what he was trying to take me to see. I turned around and headed back home. He reluctantly followed me; he was on to something, but I decided that I did not really want to find out what it was.

I saw a lot of things when I was in Memphis; it all just confirmed to me that the fallen angels are all over and have been here all along. Memphis was not different than Knoxville or Cosby. So no thanks, Teco. I have seen enough proof.

I ENJOYED VISITING WITH MY FAMILY IN MEMPHIS

The good thing about my extended stay in Memphis is that I got a chance to see many family members while I was there. However, I started to miss the liberty of being in my own space and in my own home. After about a month, I started to feel like I was intruding on a family even though Jerri never showed that in any way. But my ways were different than her ways. One thing that generally causes me a problem is too much heat, especially while sleeping. I cannot stand to be hot; Jerry loves heat, so I was always uncomfortably hot in her home. I gave her husband four hundred dollars to help with the electric bill because I knew I needed the house to be cooler. I was willing to compromise and set the air conditioning temperature to seventy-six degrees, but that was still too cold for Jerri. Each day when she came home from work, the heat went back up. Sleeping at night was a real problem for me. In the meantime, my nice, cool house was just sitting there, waiting for me.

Plus my neighbors did not know what was going on. I think Teresa knew because Ericka had called her and gave her, her side of the story. But the boys who lived on the other side of me did not know what had happened to me. They went to Teresa and asked her what had happened. Teresa told them that she thought that I had gotten sick and had to go to the hospital for a while. The boys responded very caringly and sent me get-well cards (I am sure Teresa encouraged them to do it). I was so moved by this gesture when I receive the four cards in the mail telling me how much they missed me. I knew it was time to go back home.

8

READY TO GO BACK HOME

WHILE I WAS in Memphis, Ericka never called me once to see how I was doing. She did call Jerri and tried to make her take me to the hospital to get checked out. Take me to the hospital for what? I was not sick, I do not take drugs, and no one thought my behavior was strange except for my act of rebuking demons, which we are commanded to do by our Lord, Yahushua HaMashiach (Jesus Christ).

In the meantime, while I was away from my home, my daughters decided to take control of my possessions. They took things out of my house and never told me about it. I even heard that Ericka was preparing to give my truck to Tyrone, my brother, and to have my travel trailer moved to her place. Nickole sold my car, the one I had allowed her to use because I did not need it. Mind you, Ericka never talked to me when I was in Memphis; at least Nickole did check on me and kept in contact with me. what made these girls think they could distribute my property? I wasn't dead. Ericka took the liberty to take my washer and dryer out of my house and refused to return it when I returned home. I asked her to return it. Nickole took my big-screen TV, but at least she returned a TV to me. It was her smaller TV, but that really did not bother me because my TV was too big for this small home. Other things were taken but were small and not worth mentioning.

TECO AND I FOUND A NEW FRIEND

While I was in Memphis, Jerri's dog, Chia, became attach to me. Chia could also see the entities that were in Memphis. Jerri had told me that Chia would be outside barking at something, and nobody could see what she was barking at. One day she was barking, and I looked out and saw what she was barking at. I knew what it was because I could see them, and Teco could see them also. This made Chia very happy because we understood her. She bonded with me and Teco. Teco taught her about what she was seeing and seemed to have given her a specific task to do in the watch. Teco did not bite at Chia like he did with Princess. Chia had become so attached to us that when I left, I brought her back to Cosby with me for about six weeks.

CHIA GOES HOME WITH TECO AND ME

I do believe that dogs can see and hear into the spirit realm. Teco and Chia are my proof of that. It was Teco who first saw the spirits outside of my house in April 2013, and it was Teco who Yahushua used to be like a spiritual guide dog for me. I thank my Savior for allowing me to have Teco during this time because he was my 100 percent confirmation of everything I was experiencing. Without that dog during this fiery trial, I do not know what would have kept me grounded.

People really do not understand the true intelligence of pets. They hear and see at frequency levels much higher than we humans do. What this means is that dogs, cats, and many other animals see, hear, and smell hundreds of things that humans are not aware of. In addition to seeing and hearing the presence of the fallen angels, I noticed that Teco could also smell them out. Yes, he can smell when they are around. Not only that, but Teco was able to construct representations of them. I would often see him take a paper towel and tear it into dozens of pieces and then arrange those pieces into a pattern or picture, and many times the picture that he constructed matched the call sign of one of the angels I had seen in the sky. This was a frequent practice of his, and he also taught Chia and Princess to do the same thing. Using his dog food is another way he constructed a picture. Many times, he and Princess will draw pictures or patterns using their dog nuggets as the pieces. Many times, they will go out of their way to get my attention to show me something that involves an unseen spirit. I do not always understand or get the message, but I know that they know what they are trying to communicate.

I brought Jerri's dog, Chia, home with me from my Memphis visit, and during the time that I was at Jerri's house, Teco had taught Chia many things about interacting with the spirit entities. Teco gave her a job to do, and Chia was very good at it. When she came to my house, she was right at home dealing with the spirits. I noticed she was given a certain call sign to watch out for and to alert me when she noticed that their presence was near. Remember, the dogs could see them, hear them, and smell them. I soon learned to recognize the dogs' signals that the enemy was near. Chia would demonstrate a certain behavior; this let me know they were near and where to look for their presence. I had learned to understand her language and to rebuke the spirits in that vicinity. The call sign that she watched for was the owl. These owl signs were of the fallen angels, and I had discovered that long before Chia came to visit me.

Also when I got back from Memphis, Aliyah, my granddaughter by Nickole, came over to stay with me. She was in Knoxville for the summer, and she wanted to see me. I guess all the family members had warned her that I was crazy, but she came anyway. She stayed for a few days, and we had a good time. I heard later that she told her mom that everything was normal except that the dogs, Chia and Teco, would not let her sleep on the couch. Now mind you, the dogs could see the entities, and right over the couch was a cluster of sensors. They were trying to protect her from these entities. I know they were there because they had attacked me there also. Plus she said that Gramma seemed fine, but that "rebuking stuff" was a bit scary. She went back to Maryland with her father, and everything was OK.

Chia really enjoyed herself when she was with me; she worked and enjoyed it. But keep in mind that she and Teco are dogs, and they really got on my nerves a few times. They ran off and roamed the neighborhood, which I do not allow for their own safety. People up here will shoot your dog quickly if they do not recognize it. Plus they came back stinking and full of burs and briars. After about six weeks, it was time to take Chia back home. I made the trip around my sister's birthday, which was

August 29, 2013. I drove down and took Teco and Chia with me. When we arrived, Chia was very happy to see her mom, but she never let me out of her sight. I stayed in town for a few days, and then it was time for me and Teco to head back home. Then the funniest scene occurred; we could not separate Teco and Chia. First Chia got in the car before Teco did. We said, "No, Chia, you cannot go this time." Then Teco would not get into the car. I forced Teco into the car, and then Chia got back in the car. We pulled Chia out, and Teco got out. We put Teco in, and Chia got in. This went on and on for a while until we had to pick up both dogs at the same time and separate them. It was cute, but it was sad also because they had become so attached to each other.

We finally got on the road headed back to Cosby. All went well on the trip, and we arrived home. All things were as we left them, but now Teco was alone, and he was grumpy.

9

Princess Returns Home

My asking my daughter to take Princess (my female dog) to the dog pound was the catalyst that ended up sending me on my trip to Memphis. Ericka thought that I had lost my mind. A lot of things were going on at the time, but this is the thing that pushed her over the edge. She could not imagine having Princess put to sleep. Princess was my ex-husband's mother's dog. When she died in 2009, I took the two dogs that she had owned. Their names were Teco and Princess, but it was not the same Teco I have today. Both dogs that I got from Ericka's grandmother were mixed dachshunds, brother and sister. I loved those two dogs and took them everywhere I went. But a terrible accident happened, and the first Teco was run over and killed. I was heartbroken, and Princess was heartbroken too. Princess moped around for days, and so did I because that Teco was also my buddy and was always by my side.

At that time, my daughter Nickole was working at a veterinary clinic. Her clinic provided services to dogs that the humane society picked up as strays. One day, a young dog was brought into the clinic as a stray. She said she walked back to the kennel and saw the cute dog and fell in love with it, but when she saw that his name was Teco, she knew it was sent for me. She adopted the dog and brought him to me, and we bonded. My current Teco replaced my former Teco.

In addition, before I got Teco, I had a dream where I inherited a black-and-white pig that I had to take care. I do not deal with pigs because the Bible calls them abominable and says that we are not to touch them. For this reason, I knew this dream was symbolic. Later, after getting to know Teco, I had to agree that a pig is an appropriate description of him. Like a pig, Teco will eat anything, and that can be disgusting. Teco is black and white, and he is now as fat as a pig. This dream was alerting me that Teco the pig was coming.

Back to Princess, she was Ericka's grandmother's dog, and the thought of putting her to sleep pushed my daughter off the edge. I knew that Ericka did not take the dog to the dog pound because Jurline told me so. After keeping Princess for a while, Ericka gave her to Nickole, and Princess ended up nipping one of Nickole's children. Nickole called me upset and told me that she was going to take the dog to the pound because she could not handle it. She wanted to know if I wanted her back. I said, "Yes, bring my dog home."

It was September 2013, and the attacks had lessened tremendously. I had grown spiritually, and Yahushua had taught me so much about spiritual warfare and faith. So I knew I could deal with her and Teco. Princess came home, and everything has been fine since then, which was another indication that my fiery test was over. Teco no longer attacks her, and he has taught Princess how to do spiritual warfare.

Also, I had a dream about Princess shortly before Nickole called me. I woke up one morning and heard a song by Gladys Knight, "Love Finds Its Own Way." So I guess you can say that Yahushua had already let me know that Princess would be coming home. She would be finding her way back. I never stopped loving Princess and was very happy to have her back home, but I was even happier that the spiritual attacks were just about over.

10

My Daughter Ericka and I Reconcile

WHEN I FIRST returned from Memphis, my daughter Ericka and I were still estranged; she was not talking to me. Nickole is the one who was conveying the messages concerning my washer and dryer back and forth. After I received the message that she was not going to return my stuff, I did not sweat it. Did I need more drama in my life at that point? Hardly, so I moved on. When my brother Mike was with me he left his washer and dryer in my storage. I got it out of storage and paid to have it moved and hooked up at my house; that was the end of it for me. I try not to sweat the small things.

I think this was when Yahushua took control of the situation; if anyone knew how to bring Ericka around, it was Him. He started pouring out His spirit on Amber (Ericka's daughter) and started to give her very powerful, supernatural, dreams that Ericka could not ignore. Amber started seeing angels and having dreams and visions, and Christ even spoke through her. This was totally out of the ordinary for Amber, so they had to contact me.

Ericka had Amber call me one day to tell me about the dreams and manifestations that she was having. This opened the door for Ericka. As far as I was concerned, the olive branch had always been extended, but now Ericka was extending it to get some help and understanding for her daughter. Now we could reconnect on a spiritual level, and that was the best way to get things resolved between us.

I had already forgiven her for what she did because that was the only way I could react. I believe my daughter loves me and was concerned about my wellbeing; she did not understand what was going on. I care about her soul and mine. If I allow myself to harbor any unforgiveness toward her, it could be a reason to cause her or me to stumble. We have reconciled, and that is what matters. My family is my family, and I want us all to make it into the kingdom. As for my ex-husband, Michael, as I said before, there was never any contact between us to give him a reason to do what he did. Yahushua warned me about him in the March 2013 dream; I am going to leave it at that and call it another lesson learned.

The test is not completely over for me or for any of us yet. We will all be in this competition/test/race until we leave this earth by death and resurrection, or when Yahushua comes back in His power and glory and changes our vile, wicked bodies to be like His glorified body.

Everyone will be judged and will receive their just rewards or punishments. It is not my job to seek revenge on anyone. My new husband will take care of that for me.

PART II

11

DREAMS, VISIONS, AND BIBLE STUDIES

THE FOLLOWING SECTIONS contain dreams and visions that I have had personally. In most cases, the exact date when the dream was received is noted. However, a few only have the month and year because I failed to record the date at the time of the dream.

In addition, I have included several short Bible studies on subjects that many people have questions about. The possible controversial points in these studies are confirmed by my personal revelations and experiences. All scriptures are taken from the King James Version of the bible which is in the Public Domain. I have compiled a list of Bible scriptures used in the Bible studies and the Dreams and Visions to make it easier for the reader to reference. Those Bible scriptures are compiled as the last section.

MY VISIT TO HEAVEN: I SAW GOD, THE FATHER, ON HIS THRONE

In May 2013, I had two visions of God, the Father. In the spirit, I was taken to the throne room of God by Yahushua HaMashiach,

Jesus Christ. I appeared before the Most High God of heaven and earth. I was taken there by Christ; He was in a white suit, and I was in a white dress. We were both standing before the Father; I was standing to the right of Christ. The Father was sitting high above us on a very large throne, and He seemed massive in size compared to Christ and me. We were regular human size. The Most High Father was cloaked in light, so at that time I was not able to see His face, but I felt a loving, approving spirit coming from Him, yet I was still nervous. Between the Father's throne and us there appeared to be steps made of light (cloudlike elevations leading up to Him). On my right and left I did not see any beings with my eyes, but I felt the presence of multitudes of beings all around me. It was like I was in a massive auditorium with thousands of beings alongside and above me. That vision ended.

On my next visit, I was taken to the same place and was standing in front of the Most High God with Christ by my side. Nothing was said, but all of a sudden I was taken right up to the face of God, and I looked directly into his face. He had the kindest, most loving face you can imagine, like an elderly father. The color of his face was like a dark amber stone or precious jewel. In Revelation 4:1, John describes His color as jasper and sardine (which are both dark jewel stones). He has white hair just like the Bible describes. Brothers and sisters, I have seen His color with my own spiritual eyes, and, yes when the prophets describe the Father as sardine, jasper, and dark amber, I can speak to that because I have seen it myself. His appearance is translucent, like fine jewels: almost like you can see through him.

Before my vision to the throne room, I had no idea what a jasper, sardine, beryl, or amber stoned looked like, but after my vision, I started to look for what I had seen. What I saw is consistent with what Daniel, Ezekiel, and John describe when they were allowed to see the Most High in visions.

I am sharing this vision with you because I believe that the Holy Spirit is prompting me to share this now. Please feel free to ask me any questions concerning this vision because I believe it is meant to be shared as a confirmation for Israel that He is still watching over us.

12

DREAMS AND VISIONS OF LOVE FROM YAHUSHUA TO ME

BRIDE-TO-BE ENGAGED AND BRIDE AT THE WEDDING RECEPTION

YAHUSHUA AND I ARE ENGAGED TO BE MARRIED

At about 11:30 a.m. on December 16, 2017, after waking up, I saw words written, "We are engaged," and I saw my name, Ann, written in sparkling gold letters. This was a most beautiful revelation given to me, but it was only a taste of what was to come later that night.

The first-time Yahushua showed me that we were engaged was around August 30, 2013, when I was in Memphis after taking Chia home. While the sun was setting, He created a wedding ring in the sky with the clouds and sun. He communicated this to me and had me look. I saw it and knew exactly what it meant but did not mention it to my family because they would not have understood its significance. I remembered the advice my brother Mike had given me, "You can't tell everybody everything". When I saw the ring, I just smiled and said, "Thank you my Lord". To confirm it, later on that night while I was still in Memphis, Yahushua visited me: I was all smiles all the way back to my home. I never shared that encounter; but my heart will always remember it.

THE BRIDE AND YAHUSHUA AT THE WEDDING RECEPTION

I woke at around 2:02 a.m. on the same night (December 16, 2017) and had a vision. I was the bride and saw myself standing in the receiving line at the wedding. This was the most beautiful vision; it was an awake, closed-eyed vision. It started with me seeing an image of a man with a beard and a woman coming together and kissing. Yahushua has shown me this scene many times before. This is usually shown to me in silhouette form so that I am only seeing forms and shadows with no real color to it. It is in black, gray, and white, and the figures are almost like cartoons.

As I watched these images of the man and woman kissing, the scene started to change, and suddenly I was seeing details of real people in a house/room. It was not a large area, but there were quite a few people there. I saw myself standing in front of the room in a wedding dress, and my veil was lifted. People were greeting me all around, and they seemed to be very happy to see me. I even think I saw some with small cocktail plates with food. Then I saw this Man with a crown who was seated across the room in front of me. I felt like I saw Him step down from a chair that was somewhat elevated. He came over to me, took my hands, and did a friendly head bow to me as to say, "Welcome." (Remember I was viewing this as a third person.) Then coming up from my right side I saw Yahushua with His crown walking toward me. I know it was Him because my entire being was screaming that it was Him. I saw His face, I saw His beard, and I saw that He was wearing a robe and crown. He was looking around with a very pleased expression on His face. At that point, I was so overwhelmed by what I was seeing that I might have blacked out. The vision ended, and I was left lying there in total awe of what I had just seen. Praise my King; Yahushua is amazing.

CHRIST COMES FOR HIS BRIDE

On May 22, 2016, at about 2:00 a.m., I was awakened to the most beautiful closed-eye vision you could imagine. When I woke, the first thing I saw was a heart in the sky that said "I love you." Next I saw the bust (head and shoulders) of a man and woman; they were apart but facing each other. Then I saw them moving toward each other, and they started to kiss. Next I saw what appeared to be a large Man's head hovering over everything. I knew this Man looking on represented God, the Father. After that, I saw a Man running (Yahushua). Then I saw a woman standing in the distance wearing a long, Cinderella-like dress. The Man ran toward the woman and swooped her up in His arms, and they both went up into the air. All the while, the large head of the Man in the air was looking on.

After they went up, I looked at the Man in the air (who was God, the Father), and the vision ended. It was the most beautiful thing you could ever imagine. What a perfect gift for me; I knew that the woman in the vision was me.

MOON-LIGHT LOVE FROM YAHUSHUA

On June 25, 2016, I had the most wonderful vision. I woke up at about 1:00 a.m. Nothing was going on, and I felt that things were quiet. I got up and went to the bathroom. I got back into bed but did not feel sleepy, so I thought awhile about things pertaining to me, my day and general stuff. I remember laughing to myself and saying, "Forgive me, Lord. I am so into myself that I forgot you were there." I knew He was there, but usually I am in praying mode when I wake up like that. I knew and felt that He was there all the time, but He was just observing and watching over me like He always does. I felt that He just smiled and said, "Forgiven."

I did not get on the Internet because it was not yet 2:00 a.m., so I eventually fell back asleep. I was awakened again at about 2:40 a.m. This time I prayed, praised my Lord, told him how I loved Him, and thanked Him for everything. I then looked out of my bedroom window and could see the moon coming into view. I smiled and said, "That is why you woke me" (He almost always wakes me up to see the moon when it is full). I watched the moon for a few minutes; it was high in the sky, but the night was somewhat cloudy and not very clear. Plus I was looking through slatted venetian blinds. The moon was rising higher and getting out of my view from where I was lying in bed.

It was way after 2:00 a.m. then, so I turned on my computer to see what I could watch on the Internet. There was not much there, but I watched a few short videos from a couple of watchmen I liked (watchmen are brothers and sisters watching for the signs pointing to the return of Jesus Christ). I then found a longer video and started watching it. The next thing I knew, I must have gone into vision mode because I was looking at the moon in a beautiful, dark-blue, starry sky, and everything was as clear as could be. I don't think I had fallen back to sleep because when I saw it, I was amazed at how beautiful it was. I even got up and looked out the window at the sky, but it was just like I had seen it before (cloudy). I started smiling and saying, "How did you do that?" It was like I was seeing into two dimensions (mine and His). He had performed a miracle for me so that I could see clearly. I knew He was there because I could feel His love and peacefulness (His presence is so tender, graceful, and considerate that it is hard to describe). I lay back down to see if I could see His moon again, and in just that instant I started to have a beautiful vision, which I know He gave me.

The Vision—Moon-light Love

This vision started with the moon outside. I saw the words "I love you" and the words changed to many shapes and sizes and moved in many ways; the words were alive. It was so clear that He was saying He loved me. The words then moved from the outside into my room; my eyes were closed, yet my head was moving as I watched the words change position from outside to inside. I then saw two silhouettes, a man and a woman, and they came together in an embrace and kissed. Then the Man moved across the wall of my room as I watched and followed it by moving my head (with my eyes still closed). The silhouette of the Man moved above me and came to rest right in front of my face; at that point, it was an energy mass with no discernible form. The vision ended, and I opened my eyes. I felt such joy and amazement; I was in total awe of Him.

There is no doubt that my Husband was showing His love for me. I am 100 percent sure of all the things He has promised me. To be courted by the Son of God Himself is unbelievable.

YAHUSHUA POINTS TO ME AND SAYS, "I LOVE YOU," JUNE 29, 2016

My vision that morning happened at about 3:00 a.m. I woke up, looked around my room as usual, and saw many terms of endearment written on the walls and in the air. Yes, I can see them with my physical eyes. I had a sense of peace and protection. I was a bit groggy because I had taken twenty-five milligrams of Benadryl after listening to part of the Hebrew radio network. I needed it to help me get to sleep because I really get excited when I listen to all the brothers' and sisters' testimonies. I closed my eyes again and then started to have a vision of my King.

In the air, I saw "I love you" moving all about, and then in silhouette form I saw the King in His crown and the lady again. He moved toward the lady lovingly and started to hug and kiss her as before in other visions. I saw them hugging and kissing in both an upright and a reclining position and then back in an upright position again. I have seen this vision or one like it many times, and I always knew the woman was symbolic of me, and that makes me feel good.

But this time something happened that I did not expect, and it blew my mind. All of a sudden, the King's silhouette turned and faced me, and a big, amber, glowing hand pointed a finger at me (like it came out of the spirit world into my physical realm). I heard in my spirit, "This is you. It's you." It was so real and unexpected that I just burst into laughter and thanked Him and told Him how amazing He was. Then I went to the restroom in total amazement of what had just happened. I love Him so much, and the whole world thinks I am crazy. If they only knew what I know—that no one can love you like Yahushua.

I AM COMING FOR YOU THIS WEEKEND

On March 9, 2015, in the early morning, I had a dream in which it appeared as if I were in a newsroom studio, and this man was about to interview Ben Affleck. He was saying that Ben Affleck had met someone and was already talking about getting married. The camera panned to this man sitting on the other side of the table, who I guess was Ben Affleck. I never saw him but heard him talking. He said, "I have met this person, and she is the most wonderful and different person in the world, and I am going to marry her." In the dream, I knew he was talking about me. I remember thinking, *What does "most wonderful and different" mean?* I then woke up feeling the presence of Yahushua in my room, and I even saw words of endearment written on my ceiling. I had the warmest feeling of love and a big smile on my face.

I went back to sleep and had another dream that I cannot remember, but as I woke from it, I heard in my spirit, "I am coming for you this weekend." As I was pondering that thought, I then looked into the face/presence of an energy force that made me laugh; I never heard any words spoken, but I saw Love" written in the air in many places. I felt the energy as it covered my body like a blanket and then lessened and became no longer visible to me. *Wow*, I thought. *"I am coming for you this weekend."* I knew it was my husband, Yahushua, and that He was coming for me soon.

YAHUSHUA AND THE PREGNANT WOMAN

On June 7, 2016, in the early morning, I had a short vision where I saw myself having a baby; I looked at the child in my arms and said, *Wow, I am going to have a baby.* I knew it was a boy. The vision ended. I did not think anything of it because many women have had visions of themselves being pregnant or giving birth, so I went along with my daily activities.

The next day, I was awakened at 1:00 a.m. I looked at the clock and saw the time, and then I immediately went into a vision. It was like I was looking into the clouds and sky; I saw an image of a Man dressed as a King and a woman. The King (who I knew was Yahushua) walked up to the woman and began hugging her. They were hugging each other very closely and lovingly. I could see this as a side view from the head down to the waist. The Man was taller than the woman. Then my view panned back as I saw the Man start to move and become lower than the woman. Then I noticed that the woman was pregnant. This image came into clear view, and I saw that she was very pregnant as if ready to deliver. The King, who now appeared to be on one knee, laid His head on the woman's stomach and then kissed the pregnant belly, and the woman lovingly put her hand on the King's shoulder. At that time, the vision of me giving birth came flooding into my mind, and I immediately became shaken and amazed. I lost focus on everything, and the vision ended.

I could only lie in my bed wondering about what I had just seen. I could not go back to sleep. I was up for over an hour just thinking about the vision. I asked myself the question, *Was that a vision of the Most High (Yahuwah) and His bride, Israel, or was it a vision of Yahushua and His bride, me? Or was it a vision that represented both?*

My Revelation of 2010: In 2010, it was revealed to me by the Most High that I was Israel. I was also told in 2013 that I was chosen to become the wife of Yahushua.

At that time I told my family that Yahushua told me that He was going to marry me, and of course they thought I was crazy, probably just like many of you think. But Yahushua has given me numerous dreams and visions confirming this. He has also taken me to meet the Father, and I have looked into the face of Yahuwah, the Most High God of heaven and earth. I am sharing this with you because many things are being revealed now, and He is leading me to share this with you.

Who am I? I am both the bride of Yahuwah and the wife-to-be of Yahushua HaMashiach.

THE TEST—THE BRIDE HAS GONE THROUGH THE FIRE

In the early morning of March 19, 2016, at about 2:01 a.m., I had a dream about a group of women helping me get ready for my wedding. They were rushing around, helping me to get dressed. We were in a big room, but it did not seem fancy or anything. I saw the dress that I was to put on; it was lace and appeared to have been beautiful at one time but looked like it had been through a fire. I put on all the undergarments and shoes, and it appeared that I had a red camisole on covering my chest. I started to put the dress on, and I remember wondering if it would still fit. I noticed that it was now dingy, and the lace was droopy like when washed. I proceeded to put it on, and it zipped up fine and fit. I looked in the mirror, and I could see the red color showing through the lace, and that was not good, so I thought I must find a garment that would not show through, one that was black or white. I sent one of the attendants to look for one. I continued to look in the mirror and saw that my butt looked very big in the reflection because the dress was very full around my rear as if I had gotten fat while waiting for the wedding. I woke up, but the question that stayed in my mind was: why did I have the red garment on, and why was my dress dingy and drooping?

My interpretation is that the bride had gone through the fire and had been chosen by the King to be His wife ("it was granted to her to be in fine linen"); "She will sit at his right hand as the queen" (Rev. 19:7–9, Ps. 45: 9, 11, 14).

VISITED BY ANGELS AND YAHUSHUA: TOLD THAT I WAS CHOSEN

In March 2013, I had a very vivid night vision in which I was visited by a whole host of people. There were anywhere from six to eight people in my room, including Yahushua. It was like a hospital setting, and a group of scientists came into my room and started examining me. It was like I was in a trance during all the activity. They were examining me all over, taking notes, and recording values. There was an extreme interest in my hair, and there were three or maybe four people working on my head. They were looking at it, parting my hair, taking notes, and writing things down. They seemed to have spent a lot of time around the crown of my head and the hair there. In retrospect, I think they were measuring me for my crown, and maybe they were, but my hair seemed to be of great interest.

Surprisingly, the one who I believed was Christ came into my room looking very casual in jeans rolled up to His ankles, and He did not have a shirt on.

YAHUSHUA COMES FOR ME

In April 2013, I had a dream where there was complete darkness all around. The darkness was so thick that I could hardly see in front of my face. It was biblical darkness, thick and palpable. I was standing alone in a forest or in what seemed to be a wooded area. The only light around was a campfire burning brightly next to me. I was dressed in the most beautiful cream-colored satin dress. It was long and full. My head was covered in a beautiful head covering with embroidered jewels, and it was fitted like a skull cap. There seemed to be something flowing down the backside as part of the headdress. It, too, was light-cream-colored but not white. I was standing there all alone with this large campfire illuminating my surroundings.

In the distance, I could see Christ coming around a bend in the road leading to where I was standing, yet in this dream He was quite a distance away. He was holding a lighted lamp and was headed toward me (I knew this in my spirit). I do not remember anyone else with Him, but I knew He was coming for me, and I was waiting for Him. Then I woke up.

Dream Confirmed, Dream Repeated: Several days later, I had the very same dream in the same setting, but this time Christ had made it much closer to me. In fact, Christ had made it to me; I looked into His face and gave him a big smile as our eyes met. In both dreams, I was observing myself. As Christ got closer, I smiled at Him, and He smiled at me. He had come for meat midnight. Then I woke up; the dream was over.

Prior to this dream and after, Yahushua gave me several *very* personal dreams revealing Himself to me and letting me know just who I am and what my chosen identity is. I have shared this information with all in my posts; however, there are many, many dreams and visions that Yahushua has given me personally that confirm this to me without a doubt. As I said before, I have not shared these personal dreams and visions because I felt they were private, and I still believe that. However, He is now allowing me to share these dreams and visions in this book, which I believe He is telling me now is the time to write my story.

THE CORONATION OF CHRIST (DANIEL CHAPTER 7:13-14)

On September 20, 2016, at 5:44 a.m., I was awakened by a fierce feeling of heat all over my body. I looked up toward the ceiling and saw a vision.

In the first scene, I saw just the head and shoulders of a Man. In my spirit, I knew this was Christ; He had a beard, and I knew it was Christ who I was being shown. Then I saw a tall Man's figure with a crown standing in the background. I then saw Christ kneel before this tall Man, who I knew was God, the Father. God placed a crown on Christ's head as He was kneeling before Him. While this was going on, I noticed that there was a woman standing in the background, watching everything. Christ then stood up before the Father, walked over to the woman, and gave her a hug. The vision ended.

This vision was given to me at my daughter's house the morning after I had gotten eye surgery. It reminded me of Daniel 7:13–14: "I saw in the night visions, and, behold, one like the Son of man came with the clouds of heaven, and came to the Ancient of days, and they brought him near before him. And there was given him dominion, and glory, and a kingdom, that all people, nations, and languages, should serve him: his dominion is an everlasting dominion, which shall not pass away, and his kingdom that which shall not be destroyed."

VISIONS OF WORDS

The next day, I saw words written on the ceiling saying "All power is mine," and then I saw the word Woman. I am not sure if I saw the word "all," but I think I did", He was confirming to me that I am that woman seen in the background.

13

DREAMS AND VISIONS ABOUT THE BRIDE—DARK AND DEATHLY

WEDDING RINGS AND WEDDING SCROLLS FOR THE BRIDE

AROUND APRIL 21, 2014, I had several visions that were in a very dark mode like at night. It was almost like I was seeing them in a nightlight setting. It started with me seeing a basket of white rolled-up paper like small wedding scrolls; they had beautiful golden rings around them. I got the knowledge that these scrolls were for the bride. The scene changed, and then I saw many graveyards with what appeared to be white smoke coming from the graves (like spirits going up in the air). Next I saw destruction all around like war and desolation; people were hungry and wandering around like they were lost and hopeless. Then I saw someone with his or her hands tied behind his or her back bent over a guillotine, ready to be beheaded. The dream ended.

I saw these things twice in two vision sessions on the same night, which I take as a confirmation that it was given to me by

Yahushua and that this thing will happen. This is a picture of the coming resurrection of the dead in Christ.

WEDDING PROCESSION AND FUNERAL PROCESSION

I had a dream in spring of 2013 (around May or so). It was a brief vision/dream where I saw two wedding processions. One had only one car with the bride and groom in it. The other was a long procession with many cars in it. The people were dressed in wedding attire (white). As I watched the long procession of people, it turned into a funeral procession, and in my spirit, I knew they were ALL headed for a funeral.

This dream was very disturbing to me; I wrote it down in a journal that I could not locate, but that is OK because it never left my mind; I remember it so very well. I remember thinking that the wedding was really a funeral (but we know that no flesh and blood will enter the kingdom of heaven). I also had this dream/vision twice, which I take as confirmation that this is the way it will be. I have included this dream with the one above because I think they are related. Many of God's chosen will be in the wedding/funeral procession very soon.

14

DREAMS AND VISIONS OF ISRAEL, THE PEOPLE OF GOD

DREAMS AND VISIONS ABOUT ZION AND DEALING WITH THE LEADERS OF ISRAEL

IN THE SPRING of 2013, I had a series of dreams/visions about Zion and related things. Below is one of those visions.

In this dream/vision, I was taken in the spirit through what appeared to be an opening in a mountain (a large, bonelike handle opened a door, and we entered through it). I say "we" because I knew I was being taken by Yahushua HaMashiach. There, I saw several people who were dressed like African princes; they were wearing a certain type of headdress and were dressed in what I have always associated with African dress, not Western. It was made known to me that they were elders, leaders, and princes of Israel.

At that time, there seemed to be some kind of festive occasion going on because the people were celebrating something. In a clearing surrounded by mountains, there was a tent/tabernacle. In hindsight, I believe it was the Tabernacle of David. There were not a lot of people there but enough for a celebration. Some men were excitedly carrying a man around in what looked like a chair or a throne. For some reason, I thought the man was David, but I am not sure; he was not wearing a crown (at least I do not remember a crown).

The vision zoomed in on the chair/throne, and I could see the man's large private part hanging down through the chair. I could see that it was a well-developed, circumcised black man. This was shown to me twice, so I know it must be important. I must admit that I felt very embarrassed to see it and said, "My Lord, why are you showing me this?" I repeat that I was shown this twice, so I cannot neglect to mention it. (I believe that the Most High has given me the interpretation of that part of the vision and why I was shown that particular sight.) During the vision, I was standing on the sideline watching all the festive activity from the right side of the tabernacle/tent, and Yahushua HaMashiach was with me.

In another vision, I was taken to the same place, where there were very similar activities going on.

My interpretation of these visions is as follows:

1. I was told that those were the leaders of Israel in this vision; they were all men.
2. There was a man being carried around on a throne (it was not made know to me who the man was).
3. His private parts were clearly shown to me as the object of worship.
4. The person being worshiped (being carried on the throne) could not be Christ because He was standing next to me, showing me these things.

The Israel leaders worship their maleness; it is what is sitting on their throne. I was made to know that I was going to be dealing with a hardened, well-developed/-defined, male-dominated, organizational leadership structure in Israel/Jacob but that I shouldn't worry. Christ is with me and beside me.

The message was for me, but it also applies to other women in Israel. The Most High is calling you to be bold and do His will. The message to the leaders of Israel is that the Most High is not pleased with you or this activity, and it must change.

GETTING OFF THE ROAD—WHICH WAY TO ZION?

I had a brief dream on August 19, 2016, where I was traveling down a road and thought I was going the right way. I took a turn in my car and started down the road, when suddenly the road ended, and I was driving on the grass. I knew I was off the road, so I backed up and backtracked to make sure I made the right turn, and sure enough I had taken the correct turn. Then suddenly I was running on my feet. I ran up these mountains in very rugged terrain. I met some Indian-like or desert-like people who asked me if I was lost. I told them I was trying to get to Tel Arad and to point me in that direction. They said, "Tel Arad? That place has been shut down for years," and I think I said, "I know, but which way is it from here?" They pointed the way out to me, and I continued running.

TABERNACLES BENEATH THE MOUNTAIN OF THE LORD

On April 23, 2014, I had a vision where I saw a huge mountain in the distance. The mountain was beautiful and glittering. I got the knowledge that it was the mountain of the Lord. In front of the mountain, there was a huge area of clearing, and in this clearing, there were camps/tents set up. There were tents everywhere; it reminded me of the children of Israel camped below Mount Sinai.

I was looking at the mountain from a distance; I stood on the far side of the camps and tents like I was in a cove or cleft in the rock, and very close to me were lots of people in a festive mood. I clearly saw one black man with dreadlocks wearing an apron-like outfit. This man was dancing happily, and he did a headstand right in front of me. I also plainly saw two black men with medium, short, woolly hair dressed in blue outfits and carrying streaming flags or banners. They were leaping and dancing; they did a twirl right in front of me. They were happy, I was happy, and I felt that Yahushua had brought His people together like when he brought them out of Egypt. Now as I think about it, this might have been the Feast of Tabernacles being celebrated in my vision, but I am not saying which one. Praise the most-high God of Abraham, Isaac, and Jacob.

Bobbie and the Palestinian Conflict

On August 18, 2016, I awoke at about 2:02 a.m. from a dream given to me by Yahushua. In this dream, my sister Bobbie, some other members of my family, and I were walking on a bridge. There was going to be demonstration where the Palestinian people were going to march across this bridge, and thousands of them had congregated on the bridge just behind us.

We saw them coming, so we walked quickly to cross the bridge ahead of them; it was only a few of us, maybe five or six.

As we approached the end of the bridge, we noticed hundreds of Jewish people coming and collecting there on the side to which we were crossing. I noticed they had sticks, clubs, and rocks in their hands.

As we approached, they said, "You can't come in here." We immediately said that we were not with the Palestinians, but they did not care; they were not going to allow us to cross the bridge into where they were. They were angry and ready for a fight. But we just wanted to get out of there.

Then I heard from somewhere, "There is an opening to the right of the bridge; you can escape through there." I looked to my right, and there was a small pathway beside the bridge. We ducked through the pathway from between the two groups, who were about to clash.

When we got off the bridge along the pathway, there was this small opening we had to pass through to get free. I started through the opening and got stuck; my head was stuck, my shoulders were stuck, and my hips were stuck. I remember yelling to my family to push me to unstick me, and they did.

When I was freed, I slid down a chute to a safe place. It was a nice place with paved streets and trees and grass. I did not see any people around. But because I was worried about my family, I knew I needed to go back to help get them out. I knew that because of the difficult time I had getting through the opening, my sister Bobbie was not going to try it because she weighed a bit more than me and would never make it through. But I knew I had to get them out.

So I climbed back up the chute that I slid down, and when I got to the opening, I tore it open with supernatural strength. It had an iron lattice over it, so I tore it open and ripped it into pieces so that my family could come through the opening. When I finished opening it up, I put my body through it to find my family.

At that point, the pathway had changed to a theater (a place where plays are held), and the Palestinian and Jewish people were onstage in a conflict. In addition to my family, there were other people who had congregated in a side room, not the main theater, and they were just sitting watching the play but not getting involved. I yelled to one of them, "Tell my sister Bobbie it's time to escape." That person turned around, called out Bobbie's name, and told her. I then saw Bobbie sitting in a chair; just like the rest of the people in the room, she had gotten comfortable and was watching the show.

Bobbie said to me, "I can't get through there; it's too tight." Plus she was comfortable where she was. She was also afraid to leave her comfort even though she saw that the opening was made bigger. I knew what was going on with her, so suddenly I had this very long arm, and I reached in, grabbed her, and pulled her through the opening, and we escaped to the safe place. I am sure the other family members came after her, but I did not see them. I then woke up knowing that Yahushua had given me this dream to share today.

Interpretation of the Dream

- This was a very detailed dream, but I believe Yahushua had given me a very detailed message in this dream.
- Even though I saw my biological family in this dream (my sister Bobbie), it applies to my Israelite sisters and brothers.

- The location of the dream is in Israel (Palestinians and Jewish people in conflict). My biological family has never been to Israel, but many members of my Israelite family have.

- This conflict between the Palestinian and Jewish people over the land of Israel is ongoing and is going to play itself out (that is why I saw the theater with them onstage).

- The rest of us are not involved in this conflict even though many of us have visited the land; it is not about us at this point. It is the Jewish people and the Palestinian people who are the main actors in this conflict.

- The place that the Most High has prepared for us is not in the midst of the conflict. However, we will escape through a narrow path from the conflict to a place He has prepared for us, the safe place.

- Those of us who make it through to the safe place will do so with much difficulty. Our families will be comfortable where they are and will be afraid to travel the path. It will be our job to go back and help pull our brothers and sister through to safety. This will not be by our own power, but it will be by the guidance and by the power of the Most High.

15

MISCELLANEOUS DREAMS, VISIONS, AND VISITATIONS RECEIVED OVER THE YEARS

WHITE DOVE LIFTING TO THE SKY WHILE YAHUSHUA HAMASHIACH WATCHED

ON THE MORNING of September 26, 2013, I had a dream about a beautiful white dove. First, I saw the face of Jesus lit up in the sky (white light), and in front of the face was a large spiral of glittering white light. In front of it I saw a beautiful white dove flying straight upward from the earth with its wings flapping, but it was moving upward at a smooth pace. The face of Christ was looking at the dove as if watching it and encouraging it to keep flying up. The most amazing part while in this vision was that I heard the song "On the Wings of Love" by Jeffrey Osborne. It was revealed to me that I was that white dove.

TWO VISIONS: A CORD CONNECTING GOD'S PEOPLE

I had been praying about whether I should get involved with an organization that was working on nation building. We as God's people are in many different groups, and they seem to be moving in many different directions; it really can be confusing to people who are newly waking up and want to be doing His will. Very early the following morning (March 24, 2015), I had two visions in which the Most High answered my prayer.

In my first vision, I saw several different groups of people/believers. Some of them had head coverings on, and some did not; some men had beards, and others did not; and some wore traditional clothes, while some wore more ancient types of clothing; they were all in their groups discussing the things that were important to them. However, unbeknown to them, I saw an angel (invisible to them) moving in and out among the groups. He was wrapping a thin cord around them loosely as not to inhibit them. He then moved on to the next group and did the same thing. So even though the groups did not know it, they were being connected by this angel and his cord/string. The groups did not recognize the angel, but I saw him and knew what he was doing. I believe the Most High was showing me that even though the groups appeared different, they were all His people, and He is in control of all of them. They are all connected by the cord that He has put in place, and at the appropriate time He will tighten the cord and pull everything together.

LITTLE GIRL BEING LED BY HER FATHER

On that same morning, March 24, 2015, I had another vision where I saw a wide-eyed little girl; it appeared that she was looking at me and then looking all around her at her surroundings. Then her father (a man I could only see from the shoulders down) came up and took her by her right hand and started leading her away. She happily took his hand and was being led by him, but she was still looking all around at the trees, the stream, and the sky as she was being led by her father along a path. Then the dream panned over, and I saw myself, and I knew that the little girl represented me and that the father was our heavenly Father YHWH, leading me. I also saw another person who represented the one who I have seen in visions and dreams as my angel, bending over as to be saying in a playful manner, "See? That's what I have been telling you. He is the Father; just keep your hand in His hand and follow Him." I woke up from the dream, but, yes, we must keep our hands in His and follow Him.

DIFFERENT DIMENSIONS AND REALMS

In a dream in March 2012, I and someone else (I felt it was a man) were on a road traveling somewhere, and suddenly a massive army descended from above. There were all kinds of soldiers or fighting men, lions, elephants, and fighting equipment, and they were all on the move, traveling quickly as going to battle. The man and I ducked and hid in a ditch along the road so as not to be seen by them, but I felt that they were in a different dimension. They did not see us or even know we were there. In my spirit, I knew we were in a different dimension than they were. The dream ended.

MY OUT-OF-BODY EXPERIENCE

My experience started in a dream on February 19, 2017. In the dream, I knew I had experienced a visitation from Christ where He took me in spirit somewhere and then brought me back. I knew it was like the many other times He had taken me away and brought me back, but I was not allowed to remember the experience. I know this to be true; in fact, once when I returned, He told me, "You were with me from the beginning," but I still didn't remember anything else. This time I knew I was going to remember the experience. So as I was still in the dream, I started rehearsing what had just happened so that I would not forget it. At that point in the dream, all I remembered was that Christ had just visited me and took me away again. Like before, I was asleep, and He came to me in my dream and took me away, and I later returned. I knew this had just happened, and I was trying my hardest to remember it so that when I woke up from the dream, I would be able to write it down. Then I woke up. I looked around my room, and everything seemed normal. But then I went into an amazing vision.

I saw my room open from the top, and I saw Christ as a spirit person float through the wall into my room. I was viewing this as a spectator. He floated over the bed where I was sleeping; I saw myself wake up, and this Spirit Man held out His hand to me. I took His hand (but this time it was a spirit form of me). I saw my spirit-self leave my body, and then Christ and I left my bedroom through the walls and ceiling while I watched. The vision then ended.

It was the most amazing thing I could ever imagine. It was the exact dream I had been striving to remember, but now I saw how it all happened. He had given me a vision of what I was dreaming about.

ANOTHER SHORT OUT-OF-BODY VISION
This happened to me on Friday, February 17, 2017, but I did not record this part until later because I did not understand it. I had

a vision where I came through my window and saw my body sleeping. I wondered why I was looking at myself asleep. I now know that I was again returning from an out-of-body experience with Christ and back to my body, and I was looking at myself sleeping before my spirit reunited with my body.

MY TIME WILL COME; JUST BE PATIENT AND WAIT FOR IT

On March 23, 2016, I had two very short, related dreams that I believe are personal because I really could not recognize any of the other people in it. The message is for me: just wait for it; my time is coming.

FIRST DREAM

I was in a store crowded with merchandise in the section where you buy hats. There were many people crowded around the hat stands, trying to choose a hat. They seemed to be winter hats because they were made of wool or knit material and were of dull colors like brown and gray. I wanted to buy a hat also, but I was mostly just standing back, looking at the people, and waiting until I could get to the stand to choose a hat. That was the end of that dream.

SECOND DREAM

In the other dream, I was on the outside of what seemed to be an outing of some sort like maybe a festival or a park. I was walking around alone, but I think I was eating something. People were singing in many places, and I could hear them, but at that point

I could not see them. I walked around just being outside when I came to this area where a lot of people who were singing started to converge. The singing was getting louder as they started to come together. I was standing back, looking, and snacking on something when I noticed that they all started to converge right in front of me and were looking at me lovingly. I started to look around in bewilderment when it was made known to me that they were all singing to me. *Who am I that they would be singing to me?* That was my question.

MY GIFT OF DREAMS AND DREAM INTERPRETATION: SHOES OF MANY COLORS—A GIFT FROM THE MOST HIGH

Back in 1996, the Most High gave me a vision where I saw myself putting on some shoes. When I got the vision, I knew in my spirit that I was being called for something (I felt like a prophetess, but I dismissed it). Anyway, the shoes were old fashioned-looking and not anything I wanted to wear, so I forgot about the dream and went on with my life. Yet I always remembered them and joked about the "ugly shoes" to my family members with whom I had shared the dream.

Back in 2012, I had another vision where I received a gift in the spirit, and in the box was a beautiful pair of shoes of many colors. They were made from fine-textured, sparkling cloth. In my spirit, I was told that they were like Joseph's coat of many colors. I knew that the Lord was giving me the gift of dreams and dream interpretation like Joseph had. But I laughed because I also knew that with His sense of humor, He was chiding me for complaining about the "ugly shoes." So as this new gift, He gave me these beautiful shoes, which represented my gift of dream interpretation. He does have a sense of humor.

PUTTING MY SHOES ON

I had a dream on July 31, 2015. I was outside sitting on some steps with a child, and I was putting on my shoes as if I was getting ready to run. I told the child to go back into the house and find the rest of family members because she would not be able to run. Then I saw myself running up this long road; it was somewhat rocky and sort of dark and on a steady incline. I was running fast, and I saw this opening in the dark, but it was still a distance in front. The opening was partially open or partially closed (I'm not sure), but I knew I had to get to it and through it to be able to escape. I woke up before getting to the opening.

My interpretation is that I believe this pertains to the coming Second Exodus. All the children will not go; some will stay behind. It will not be an easy run, and it appears that it will be a lengthy road, but the escape way is open, and the run is about to begin, so put your shoes on if you are planning to go.

I HAVE GIVEN YOU ALL YOU NEED TO CONQUER SATAN: NOW USE IT

I remember when I was having my trials in 2013, I was constantly being attacked by Satan and demonic forces. They would appear to me in all forms and torment me. They were relentless, every day and night I was being afflicted. The only weapon I knew was to rebuke them in the name of Yahushua. Christ kept telling me to rebuke them. I would rebuke them all and they will flee: Yes, they did flee but they would always return. I started doubting that I was doing all I could be doing, so I started researching the internet trying to find ways to rebuke the devil; Ways to do spiritual warfare. I remember I sought out books on demons, fairies, Djinns, and other demonic spirit beings.

I watched videos on aliens and other unidentified entities. I studied how demons manifested and attacked people: I tried to learn all types of special prayers being taught on how to rebuke demons, and how to anoint my home. I even read one place where it advocated the use of bells that emitted a certain frequency sound which would run them off. The book said brass bells emitted sounds that they didn't like, I took note of that. I also found out that certain incenses would ward them off. I knew that the priests in the Bible burned incense and rung bells, so I went out and bought some incense: Frankincense and Myrrh. I already owned a brass tea set with pitcher and cups.

So I converted a couple of the cups into bells so I could ring them while burning the incense. I was serious about my intentions, but it did not help at all.

Then one night, my room lit up like an electrical storm. It was not bright but like sound waves that I could see with my eyes: A massive electrical being came into my presence. I knew it was God the Father. I just knew it, there is no way I can explain it, except to say, I knew it was him. He spoke to my mind, He said, "daughter I see and hear you. I have given you everything you need to rebuke them. I have given you the Name above all Names. Now use it". Then the powerful presence moved past me. I lay there knowing exactly what he meant. That put an end to all the books and outside research I was doing. That is exactly what the bible teaches. There is no name higher than Yahushua HaMashiach, Jesus Christ. His visit gave me the confidence I needed. I did not need to seek out council from any other source. He has already given us everything we need; we just need to use it. I started rebuking everything that popped up. These are the words I use. They work for me because I have faith in the Name that is behind my words.

"I rebuke you in the name of Yahushua HaMashiach, and by the power of the Ruach HaKadash. I call on the father, Yahuwah to send his holy angel to my aid to destroy all evil entities in my presence. And if there is anything that is not of Yahushua, I demand you to leave my presence immediately. You are not invited nor are you welcome here. I am covered by the blood of Yahushua HaMashiach who died for me on the cross of Calvary. I rebuke you in the name of Jesus Christ of Nazareth. Leave my presence and do not return. I bind you and send you back to the pit of hell where you belong; in the Name of Yahushua HaMashiach."

16

SHORT TEACHINGS ON MARRIAGE IN THE KINGDOM

MARRIAGE, SEX, AND CHILDBIRTH IN THE MILLENNIUM KINGDOM
THE GENESIS CURSE ON WOMEN WILL BE OVER FOR THOSE IN THE KINGDOM

*Unto the woman he said, I will greatly multiply thy
sorrow and thy conception; in sorrow, thou shalt
bring forth children; and thy desire shall be to thy
husband, and he shall rule over thee.*

—GENESIS 3:16

CHRIST AND HIS Glorified Body: Christ will return in a physical body, one with all the male parts of the normal human being. When Christ returns in power and glory, He will have the same resurrected body He had when we walked this earth over two thousand years ago. It is a flesh-and-bone body but glorified. It is not a spirit body (Luke 24:39, Acts 1:11, John 20:17). He will eat and drink like we do now (Luke 24:42). He will marry, have sex, and have children. Childbirth for women will not be painful like it is now because the Genesis 3:16 "curse" will be over.

A REVELATION THAT MANY DO NOT UNDERSTAND AND FIND HARD TO BELIEVE

A lot of people do not understand that there will be marriage in the kingdom of God, and children will be born in the new kingdom.

In Matthew 22:30, Christ said that those who are resurrected will not marry or be given in marriage; however, He never said anything about those who will enter the kingdom without dying. In 1 Corinthians 15:51, 52, Paul said that we shall not all die, but we shall all be changed. Those who are changed (who did not die) are not part of the resurrection, and they will be able to procreate.

In Isaiah 65:17–20, we see children being born and people dying. We know that this will happen in the millennium because after the thousand-year reign of Christ, death will be destroyed but *not* until after the millennial reign of Christ.

Yahushua Will Have Sons: In Ezekiel 46: 12, 16, the Prince in the millennium is Christ. It cannot be King David because King David will be resurrected, and he will not marry nor have children (Matt. 22:30). This verse is talking about Yahushua, who is the King's Son, the Prince (Matt. 22:2, 3). Notice again in Ezekiel 46:18 that the prince has sons (children are being born to the married prince).

WEDDING PARABLES

There are three main parables that talk about Yahushua getting married. I have already shown that there will be babies born in God's kingdom. The three parables are as follow:

1. The midnight cry (Matt. 25)
2. The Father prepares a wedding for His Son (Matt. 22)
3. The watchmen after the wedding (Luke 12: 36–38)

Remember that Christ is the Second Adam. He will restore all things to as they were before the fall of man, and He will have children (1 Cor. 15:45).

Yahushua Will Choose a Woman to Be His Wife: The King, God the Father, Is making a marriage for His Son, Yahushua HaMashiach, Jesus Christ. King Yahushua is going to take a human woman to be His wife, His queen. This is different from the New Jerusalem, which is the Lamb's wife or bride. Yahushua will marry a woman; she will be the queen, and she will stand on His right side (Ps. 45:9–14, Isa. 62:5, Mark 10:38–41).

Other Scriptures Referring to the King's Marriage:

The Story in Mark 10:38–41: Remember the story where James and John, the sons of Zebedee, asked Christ if they could sit on His right side and His left side when He comes into His glory/kingdom? Jesus said to them, "You don't know what you are asking for: Can you drink of the cup that I drink of and be baptized with the baptism that I am baptized with?" James and John said they could drink from the cup. Christ said, "Indeed you will drink of the cup as you said: But this position to sit on my right and left is not mine to give but will be given to them whom it was prepared for." If you read Psalm 45:9, it clearly states that the queen will stand on the right side of Christ, the King; obviously, that spot was prepared for the queen.

Psalm 45:9–14: Kings' daughters were among thy honorable women: upon thy right hand did stand the queen in gold of Ophir. Hearken, O daughter, and consider, and incline thine ear; forget also thine own people, and thy father's house; so shall the king greatly desire thy beauty: for he is thy Lord; and worship thou him. The king's daughter is all glorious within: her clothing is of wrought gold. She shall be brought unto the king in raiment of needlework: the virgins her companions that follow her shall be brought unto thee.

    Isaiah 62:5: For as a young man marries a virgin, so shall thy sons marry thee: and as the bridegroom rejoices over the bride, so shall thy God rejoice over thee.

THE CHURCH IS NOT THE BRIDE
THE CHURCH IS THE BODY OF CHRIST

There is not a single scripture in the Bible that teaches that the Church is the wife of Christ, nor does it say that the Church is the bride of Christ. The bride of Christ is taken from the "righteous saints" of God, from the Body of Christ like Eve was taken from the body of Adam.

- The Church is the body of Christ (2 Cor. 11:2, Eph. 5:25–33, Matt. 9:14, 15). The Lamb of God (Yahushua) will choose a wife from among the "righteous saints" (Rev. 19:7). The Lamb's wife has made herself ready for marriage. How has she made herself ready? Revelation 19:8 tells us, "And to her was granted that she should be arrayed in fine linen, clean and white: for the fine linen is the righteousness of the saints."

- Yahushua is a person; He was born into this world as a Son of man. He is going to marry a daughter of Zion. I have been told by Yahushua HaMashiach that He is going to marry me. He told me this many, many times and has given me many, many dreams and visions to confirm this.

- The Church is an organizational body. Christ loves the Church like a man should love his wife; this is not saying that the Church is Yahushuas wife. He has given many visions to watchmen over and over again showing that the King's wife is a woman, but men and women choose to ignore what the Bible is saying so that they can continue their fanciful tales.

- King Yahushua has promised me that He is going to marry me. I did not grow up in a church that taught the bride doctrine; I learned about it in 2013, when it was revealed to me that I was chosen to be the wife of Yahushua HaMashiach (Jesus Christ).

- People must understand that the only way you can be fooled and disappointed is when you choose to believe something that is not true. Many Christians are choosing to continue to believe that the Church is the bride when the Bible clearly teaches that the Church is the Body of Christ.

- Consider Adam and Eve. Just as Adam, the first man, received his wife, Eve, by having one of his ribs removed so that she became his wife, Christ, the Second Adam, will choose His wife. I have been a faithful member of the Body of Christ, and I have been told that I am the chosen wife. I praise Yahushua every day for choosing me. I humbly understand that there is nothing in me that makes me worthy of this great honor; it is only by His grace and mercy that I was chosen.

WHO IS THE WIFE OF CHRIST/YAHUSHUA?

She has gone through the fire and was chosen by the King to be His wife ("it was granted to her to be in fine linen"); "she will sit at His right hand as the queen" (Ps. 45: 9, 11, 14).

I can attest that I have gone through fire; this book is evidence of that. When my test and trials were going on, I had no idea what was happening to me. But I passed the test, because Yahushua has told me that I will be the queen.

The King has chosen His wife. The King has granted this to me; it was not of my own worth ("it was granted to her to be in fine linen," Rev. 19). The chosen "will sit at his right hand as the queen" (Ps. 45: 9, 11, 14).

THE MEANING OF BEULAH

Beulah as a girl's name is pronounced "BYOO-lah." It is of Hebrew origin, and the meaning of Beulah is "bride." It is a biblical name symbolic of the heavenly Zion. It is used to refer to Israel, and in John Bunyan's *The Pilgrim's Progress*, Beulah is the promised land. It is a name applied to the land of Israel or Jerusalem, possibly as denoting its future prosperity (Isa. 62:4).

A MESSAGE GIVEN TO ME BY YAHUSHUA

In April 2013, I woke hearing a song that I had never heard before; it was about Beulah Land. I then heard a word from Yahushua that said, "You are my Beulah, Beulah." Then the next night when I awoke, I heard, "Girl, you are the best thing that has ever happened to me." He called me His woman; he has often told me, "You are my woman."

Isaiah 62:4 states, Thou shalt no more be termed Forsaken; neither shall thy land any more be termed Desolate: but thou shalt be called Hephzi-bah, and thy land Beulah: for the LORD delighteth in thee, and thy land shall be married.

17

Bible Scriptures and Text Used—King James Version

THE FOLLOWING SECTION contains a compilation of Bible text used in the short Bible studies as well as those referenced in the Dreams and Vision section. All scripture text is taken from the King James Bible which is in the Public Domain. I have compiled this list of Bible scriptures being used in an effort to make it easier for the reader to reference Bible text.

Version Information

In 1604, King James I of England authorized that a new translation of the Bible into English be started. It was finished in 1611, just 85 years after the first translation of the New Testament into English appeared (Tyndale, 1526). The Authorized Version, or King James Version, quickly became the standard for English-speaking Protestants. Its flowing language and prose rhythm has had a profound influence on the literature of the past 400 years. The King James Version present on the Bible Gateway matches the 1987 printing. The KJV is public domain in the United States.

Matthew 9:14, 15: Then came to him the disciples of John, saying, Why do we and the Pharisees fast oft, but thy disciples fast not? 15 And Jesus said unto them, Can the children of the bridechamber mourn, as long as the bridegroom is with them? but the days will come, when the bridegroom shall be taken from them, and then shall they fast.

Matthew 22: And Jesus answered and spake unto them again by parables, and said,

2 The kingdom of heaven is like unto a certain king, which made a marriage for his son, 3 And sent forth his servants to call them that were bidden to the wedding: and they would not come. 4 Again, he sent forth other servants, saying, Tell them which are bidden, Behold, I have prepared my dinner: my oxen and my fatlings are killed, and all things are ready: come unto the marriage. 5 But they made light of it, and went their ways, one to his farm, another to his merchandise: 6 And the remnant took his servants, and entreated them spitefully, and slew them. 7 But when the king heard thereof, he was wroth: and he sent forth his armies, and destroyed those murderers, and burned up their city. 8 Then saith he to his servants, The wedding is ready, but they which were bidden were not worthy. 9 Go ye therefore into the highways, and as many as ye shall find, bid to the marriage. 10 So those servants went out into the highways, and gathered together all as many as they found, both bad and good: and the wedding was furnished with guests.

11 And when the king came in to see the guests, he saw there a man which had not on a wedding garment: 12 And he saith

unto him, Friend, how camest thou in hither not having a wedding garment? And he was speechless. 13 Then said the king to the servants, Bind him hand and foot, and take him away, and cast him into outer darkness, there shall be weeping and gnashing of teeth.14 For many are called, but few are chosen. 15 Then went the Pharisees, and took counsel how they might entangle him in his talk.16 And they sent out unto him their disciples with the Herodians, saying, Master, we know that thou art true, and teachest the way of God in truth, neither carest thou for any man: for thou regardest not the person of men.17 Tell us therefore, What thinkest thou? Is it lawful to give tribute unto Caesar, or not?18 But Jesus perceived their wickedness, and said, Why tempt ye me, ye hypocrites?19 Shew me the tribute money. And they brought unto him a penny.20 And he saith unto them, Whose is this image and superscription?21 They say unto him, Caesar's. Then saith he unto them, Render therefore unto Caesar the things which are Caesar's; and unto God the things that are God's.22 When they had heard these words, they marvelled, and left him, and went their way. 23 The same day came to him the Sadducees, which say that there is no resurrection, and asked him,24 Saying, Master, Moses said, If a man die, having no children, his brother shall marry his wife, and raise up seed unto his brother. 25 Now there were with us seven brethren: and the first, when he had married a wife, deceased, and, having no issue, left his wife unto his brother:26 Likewise the second also, and the third, unto the seventh.27 And last of all the woman died also. 28 Therefore in the resurrection whose wife shall she be of the seven? for they all had her. 29 Jesus answered and said unto them, Ye do err, not knowing the scriptures, nor the power of God. 30 For in the resurrection they neither marry, nor are given in marriage, but are as the angels of God in heaven.31 But as touching the resurrection of the dead, have ye not read that which was spoken unto you by God, saying, 32 I am the God of Abraham, and the God of Isaac, and the God of Jacob? God is not the God of the dead, but of the living. 33 And when the multitude heard this, they were astonished at his doctrine.34 But when the Pharisees had heard that he had put the Sadducees to silence, they were gathered together. 35 Then one of them, which was a lawyer, asked him a question, tempting him, and saying, 36 Master, which is the great commandment in the law? 37 Jesus said unto him, Thou shalt love the Lord thy God with all thy heart, and with all thy soul, and with all thy mind. 38 This is the first and great commandment. 39 And the second is like unto it, Thou shalt love thy neighbour as thyself. 40 On these two commandments hang all the law and the prophets. 41 While the Pharisees were gathered together, Jesus asked them, 42 Saying, What think ye of Christ? whose son is he? They say unto him, The son of David. 43 He saith unto them, How then doth David in spirit call him Lord, saying,44 The Lord said unto my Lord, Sit thou on my right hand, till I make thine enemies thy footstool?

45 If David then call him Lord, how is he his son? 46 And no man was able to answer him a word, neither durst any man from that day forth ask him any more questions.

Matthew 25: Then shall the kingdom of heaven be likened unto ten virgins, which took their lamps, and went forth to meet the bridegroom. 2 And five of them were wise, and five were foolish.3 They that were foolish took their lamps, and took no oil with them:4 But the wise took oil in their vessels with their lamps. 5 While the bridegroom tarried, they all slumbered and slept. 6 And at midnight there was a cry made, Behold, the bridegroom cometh; go ye out to meet him.7 Then all those virgins arose, and trimmed their lamps. 8 And the foolish said unto the wise, Give us of your oil; for our lamps are gone out.9 But the wise answered, saying, Not so; lest there be not enough for us and you: but go ye rather to them that sell, and buy for yourselves.

10 And while they went to buy, the bridegroom came; and they that were ready went in with him to the marriage: and the door was shut. 11 Afterward came also the other virgins, saying, Lord, Lord, open to us.12 But he answered and said, Verily I say unto you, I know you not.13 Watch therefore, for ye know neither the day nor the hour wherein the Son of man cometh. 14 For the kingdom of heaven is as a man travelling into a far country, who called his own servants, and delivered unto them his goods. 15 And unto one he gave five talents, to another two, and to another one; to every man according to his several ability; and straightway took his journey. 16 Then he that had received the five talents went and traded with the same, and made them other five talents. 17 And likewise he that had received two, he also gained other two. 18 But he that had received one went and digged in the earth, and hid his lord's money. 19 After a long time the lord of those servants cometh, and reckoneth with them. 20 And so he that had received five talents came and brought other five talents, saying, Lord, thou deliveredst unto me five talents: behold, I have gained beside them five talents more.

21 His lord said unto him, Well done, thou good and faithful servant: thou hast been faithful over a few things, I will make thee ruler over many things: enter thou into the joy of thy lord. 22 He also that had received two talents came and said, Lord, thou deliveredst unto me two talents: behold, I have gained two other talents beside them. 23 His lord said unto him, Well done, good and faithful servant; thou hast been faithful over a few things, I will make thee ruler over many things: enter thou into the joy of thy lord. 24 Then he which had received the one talent came and said, Lord, I knew thee that thou art an hard man, reaping where thou hast not sown, and gathering where thou hast not strawed:25 And I was afraid, and went and hid thy talent in the earth: lo, there thou hast that is thine. 26 His lord answered and said unto him, Thou wicked and slothful servant, thou knewest that I reap where I sowed not, and gather where I have not strawed: 27 Thou oughtest therefore to have put my money to the exchangers, and then at my coming I should have received mine own with usury. 28 Take therefore the talent from him, and give it unto him which hath ten talents. 29 For unto every one that hath shall be given, and he shall have abundance: but from him that hath not shall be taken away even that which he hath. 30 And cast ye the unprofitable servant into outer darkness: there shall be weeping and gnashing of teeth. 31 When the Son of man shall come in his glory, and all the holy angels with him, then shall he sit upon the throne of his glory:

32 And before him shall be gathered all nations: and he shall separate them one from another, as a shepherd divideth his sheep from the goats: 33 And he shall set the sheep on his right hand, but the goats on the left. 34 Then shall the King say unto them

on his right hand, Come, ye blessed of my Father, inherit the kingdom prepared for you from the foundation of the world: 35 For I was an hungred, and ye gave me meat: I was thirsty, and ye gave me drink: I was a stranger, and ye took me in: 36 Naked, and ye clothed me: I was sick, and ye visited me: I was in prison, and ye came unto me.

37 Then shall the righteous answer him, saying, Lord, when saw we thee an hungred, and fed thee? or thirsty, and gave thee drink? 38 When saw we thee a stranger, and took thee in? or naked, and clothed thee?39 Or when saw we thee sick, or in prison, and came unto thee? 40 And the King shall answer and say unto them, Verily I say unto you, Inasmuch as ye have done it unto one of the least of these my brethren, ye have done it unto me. 41 Then shall he say also unto them on the left hand, Depart from me, ye cursed, into everlasting fire, prepared for the devil and his angels: 42 For I was an hungred, and ye gave me no meat: I was thirsty, and ye gave me no drink:

43 I was a stranger, and ye took me not in: naked, and ye clothed me not: sick, and in prison, and ye visited me not. 44 Then shall they also answer him, saying, Lord, when saw we thee an hungred, or athirst, or a stranger, or naked, or sick, or in prison, and did not minister unto thee? 45 Then shall he answer them, saying, Verily I say unto you, Inasmuch as ye did it not to one of the least of these, ye did it not to me. 46 And these shall go away into everlasting punishment: but the righteous into life eternal.

Mark 10:38 - 40: But Jesus said unto them, Ye know not what ye ask: can ye drink of the cup that I drink of? and be baptized with the baptism that I am baptized with? 39 And they said unto him, We can. And Jesus said unto them, Ye shall indeed drink of the cup that I drink of; and with the baptism that I am baptized withal shall ye be baptized: 40 But to sit on my right hand and on my left hand is not mine to give; but it shall be given to them for whom it is prepared.

Luke 12:36–38: And ye yourselves like unto men that wait for their lord, when he will return from the wedding; that when he cometh and knocketh, they may open unto him immediately. Blessed [are] those servants, whom the lord when he cometh shall find watching: verily I say unto you, that he shall gird himself, and make them to sit down to meat, and will come forth and serve them. And if he shall come in the second watch, or come in the third watch, and find [them] so, blessed are those servants.

Luke 24:39: Behold my hands and my feet, that it is I myself: handle me, and see; for a spirit hath not flesh and bones, as ye see me have.

Luke 24:42: And they gave him a piece of a broiled fish, and of an honeycomb.

John 20:17: Jesus saith unto her, Touch me not; for I am not yet ascended to my Father: but go to my brethren, and say unto them, I ascend unto my Father, and your Father; and [to] my God, and your God.

Acts 1:11: Which also said, Ye men of Galilee, why stand ye gazing up into heaven? this same Jesus, which is taken up from you into heaven, shall so come in like manner as ye have seen him go into heaven.

1 Corinthians 15:45: And so it is written, The first man Adam was made a living soul; the last Adam [was made] a quickening spirit.

1 Corinthians 15:51–52: Behold, I shew you a mystery; We shall not all sleep, but we shall all be changed, In a moment, 52 in the twinkling of an eye, at the last trump: for the trumpet shall sound, and the dead shall be raised incorruptible, and we shall be changed.

2 Corinthians 11:2: For I am jealous over you with godly jealousy: for I have espoused you to one husband, that I may present [you as] a chaste virgin to Christ.

Ephesians 5:25–33: Husbands, love your wives, even as Christ also loved the church, and gave himself for it; 26 That he might sanctify and cleanse it with the washing of water by the word, 27 That he might present it to himself a glorious church, not having spot, or wrinkle, or any such thing; but that it should be holy and without blemish. 28 So ought men to love their wives as their own bodies. He that loveth his wife loveth himself. 29 For no man ever yet hated his own flesh; but nourisheth and cherisheth it, even as the Lord the church: 30 For we are members of his body, of his flesh, and of his bones. 31 For this cause shall a man leave his father and mother, and shall be joined unto his wife, and they two shall be one flesh. 32 This is a great mystery: but I speak concerning Christ and the church. 33 Nevertheless let every one of you in particular so love his wife even as himself; and the wife see that she reverence her husband.

Revelation 19:7: Let us be glad and rejoice, and give honour to him: for the marriage of the Lamb is come, and his wife hath made herself ready.

Revelation 19:8: And to her was granted that she should be arrayed in fine linen, clean and white: for the fine linen is the righteousness of saints.

Revelation 21:2: And I John saw the holy city, new Jerusalem, coming down from God out of heaven, prepared as a bride adorned for her husband.

Revelation 21:9: And there came unto me one of the seven angels which had the seven vials full of the seven last plagues, and talked with me, saying, Come hither, I will shew thee the bride, the Lamb's wife.

Revelation 22:3: And there shall be no more curse: but the throne of God and of the Lamb shall be in it; and his servants shall serve him.

Genesis 3:16: Unto the woman he said, I will greatly multiply thy sorrow and thy conception; in sorrow thou shalt bring forth children; and thy desire [shall be] to thy husband, and he shall rule over thee.

Isaiah 62:4, 5: Thou shalt no more be termed Forsaken; neither shall thy land any more be termed Desolate: but thou shalt be called Hephzibah, and thy land Beulah: for the LORD delighteth in thee, and thy land shall be married. For [as] a young man marrieth a virgin, [so] shall thy sons marry thee: and [as] the bridegroom rejoiceth over the bride, [so] shall thy God rejoice over thee.

Isaiah 65:17–22: For, behold, I create new heavens and a new earth: and the former shall not be remembered, nor come into mind.18 But be ye glad and rejoice for ever in that which I create: for, behold, I create Jerusalem a rejoicing, and her people a joy. 19 And I will rejoice in Jerusalem, and joy in my people: and the voice of weeping shall be no more heard in her, nor the voice of crying. 20 There shall be no more thence an infant of days, nor an old man that hath not filled his days: for the child shall die an hundred years old; but the sinner being an hundred years old shall be accursed. 21 And they shall build houses, and inhabit them; and they shall plant vineyards, and eat the fruit of them. 22 They shall not build, and another inhabit; they shall not plant, and another eat: for as the days of a tree are the days of my people, and mine elect shall long enjoy the work of their hands.

Ezekiel 46: 12–18: Now when the prince shall prepare a voluntary burnt offering or peace offerings voluntarily unto the Lord, one shall then open him the gate that looketh toward the east, and he shall prepare his burnt offering and his peace offerings, as he did on the sabbath day: then he shall go forth; and after his going forth one shall shut the gate. 13 Thou shalt daily prepare a burnt offering unto the Lord of a lamb of the first year without blemish: thou shalt prepare it every morning. 14 And thou shalt prepare a meat offering for it every morning, the sixth part of an ephah, and the third part of an hin of oil, to temper with the fine flour; a meat offering continually by a perpetual ordinance unto the Lord. 15 Thus shall they prepare the lamb, and the meat offering, and the oil, every morning for a continual burnt offering. 16 Thus saith the Lord God; If the prince give a gift unto any of his sons, the inheritance thereof shall be his sons'; it shall be their possession by inheritance. 17 But if he give a gift of his inheritance to one of his servants, then it shall be his to the year of liberty; after it shall return to the prince: but his inheritance shall be his sons' for them. 18 Moreover the prince shall not take of the people's inheritance by oppression, to thrust them out of their possession; but he shall give his sons inheritance out of his own possession: that my people be not scattered every man from his possession.

Psalms 45:9–15: 9 Kings' daughters were among thy honourable women: upon thy right hand did stand the queen in gold of Ophir. 10 Hearken, O daughter, and consider, and incline thine ear; forget also thine own people, and thy father's house;

11 So shall the king greatly desire thy beauty: for he is thy Lord; and worship thou him. 12 And the daughter of Tyre shall be there with a gift; even the rich among the people shall intreat thy favour. 13 The king's daughter is all glorious within: her clothing is of wrought gold.14 She shall be brought unto the king in raiment of needlework: the virgins her companions that follow her shall be brought unto thee.

15 With gladness and rejoicing shall they be brought: they shall enter into the king's palace.

Song of Solomon 2:16: My beloved is mine, and I am his: he feedeth among the lilies.

ABOUT THE AUTHOR

Annie Sipp Blackwell is a dedicated follower of Yahushua HaMashiach (Jesus Christ) and was first baptized at eleven years old, but like most young people, she briefly strayed away. However, by the grace of God and His unfailing mercy, He drew her back to Him.

She grew up in a large African American family in the small town of Coldwater, Mississippi, with her father, mother, six brothers, and three sisters. Her mother is a beautiful, hardworking woman, and her father was a strong, even harder-working Christian man (now deceased). She attended Tuskegee University in Tuskegee, Alabama, and majored in Mathematics. She was married to Michael Blackwell, with whom she had two beautiful daughters Ericka and Nickole. She also attended Johns Hopkins University of Baltimore, Maryland, and received a double master in Technical Project Management. She now resides in Cosby, Tennessee, and is still faithfully following the leading of her Lord and Savior, Yahushua HaMashiach (Jesus Christ).

This is the author's first published book. This book was deeply inspired by and records the supernatural experiences that the author went through from February 2013 to September 2013. Since that time, the author has had many dreams, visions, and revelations from God that she may publish in subsequent books if she is inspired and led to by Yahushua HaMashiach, the King.

ABOUT THE AUTHOR

Annie Sipp Blackwell is a longtime believer in Jesus Christ—also known as Yahushua HaMashiach. She was first baptized as a young girl, but after straying from Him for a brief period, He offered His grace and drew her to Him once again.

Annie Sipp Blackwell

Blackwell is part of a large African American family and grew up in Mississippi. She attended Tuskegee University in Alabama, where she majored in mathematics. She also received a double master's degree in technical project management from Johns Hopkins University.

Blackwell married and had two daughters: Ericka and Nickole. She currently lives in Cosby, Tennessee, and continues to enjoy life as a devoted follower of her savior, Yahushua HaMashiach.

Beyond Intimacy with Yahushua, Jesus Christ: Full Disclosure of My Fiery Trials to Be His Wife is Blackwell's first book, and it was inspired by an incredible true-life encounter in 2013.

My Personal Handwritten Statement
Declaring the Events in this Book are True.

Annie Sipp Blackwell
Cosby, TN
May 12, 2017

I, Annie Sipp Blackwell solemnly swear that the testimony written in this book concerning my 2013 supernatural encounters - February - September 2013, were my true-life experiences.

Nothing was fabricated, exaggerated, or made up. Every event happened as reported. My story is one where real-life events were stranger than fiction, that is why I decided to include this hand-written statement.

In addition, all dreams and visions recorded in the book were given to me and were recorded as accurately as I remembered.

I was told by Yahushua Hamashiach, Jesus, Christ, to write this book. He was involved in every step of the process. This is his will, I am just an obedient servant.

Annie Sipp Blackwell

ABOUT THE BOOK

They came into the room and took control of everything—six to eight of what appeared to be medical staff members and scientists. They examined her, took measurements, and recorded values. They seemed extremely interested in her hair; they parted it, looked at it, took samples, and measured her head around the crown area. She was told that she was chosen to marry King Yahushua, Jesus Christ. She was told that the King was in the room. Then she remembered an unusual dream she had the previous month wherein a Man entered her bedroom wearing only a sword on His right side and left her with the most amazing, ecstatic experience she had ever known. In the dream, she knew that Man was her new Husband—and now this. She was confused. Why was she now seeing and hearing things she had never experienced before? Why were spaceships and spacecraft now visible outside of her house? Why was her house being scanned by aliens and her DNA being sought out? Why was she being pursued by aliens and demons?

This is how the fiery trials began for the woman chosen to marry Yahushua, Jesus Christ. This book chronicles her experience. She never knew what being chosen meant; she never imagined the trials that came along with it. Like Jesus Christ, she had a cross to bear. Her home was invaded by aliens; she was almost abducted by Satan, almost thrown into a mental hospital, betrayed by her family, and taken to heaven, where she looked into the face of God. She overcame fear with faith and was told that she had been selected to sit at the right hand of King Yahushua and be His queen. This is the story of the woman chosen to be the wife of Yahushua, Jesus Christ.

www.ingramcontent.com/pod-product-compliance
Lightning Source LLC
Chambersburg PA
CBHW071753090426
42737CB00012B/1806